THE CRAFT OF
EFFECTIVE LETTER WRITING

Also by Gordon Wells:

The Magazine Writer's Handbook
The Book Writer's Handbook
The Craft of Writing Articles
Writers' Questions Answered

The Successful Author's Handbook

How to Communicate

Other Allison & Busby "Writers' Guides":

How to Write Stories for Magazines by Donna Baker
The Craft of Novel-Writing by Dianne Doubtfire
How to Publish Your Poetry by Peter Finch
How to Publish Yourself by Peter Finch
The Craft of TV Copywriting by John Harding
How to Write for Children by Tessa Krailing
Dear Author . . . by Michael Legat
The Craft of Writing Romance by Jean Saunders
Writing Step by Step by Jean Saunders
The Craft of Writing TV Comedy by Lew Schwarz
How to Write for Teenagers by David Silwyn Williams

The Craft of Effective Letter Writing

A practical guide

Gordon Wells

Allison & Busby
Published by W. H. Allen & Co. Plc

An Allison & Busby book
Published in 1989 by
W. H. Allen & Co. Plc
Sekforde House
175/9 St John Street
London EC1V 4LL

Copyright © 1989 by Gordon Wells

Set in Times by Input Typesetting Ltd, London
Printed in Great Britain by
Cox & Wyman Ltd, Reading, Berks

ISBN 0 85031 933 1

This book is sold subject to the condition that it shall
not, by way of trade or otherwise, be lent, re-sold, hired
out or otherwise circulated without the publisher's prior
consent in any form of binding or cover other than that in
which it is published, and without a similar condition including
this condition being imposed upon the subsequent purchaser.

CONTENTS

Introduction   1

The Effective letter. Other writings.

1   The Planning Stage   5

The reader. The purpose. The content. The structure.
Longer documents. Word budgets. Headings.
Summary.

2   Writing Style   25

Transparent writing. Writing simply. Short simple
words. Short simple sentences. Short paragraphs.
Simple punctuation. Writing tone. Actual writing.
Polishing. Other checks. Summary.

3   Everyday Letters   43

Seeking help or information. Selling yourself.
Responding to job advertisements. Seeking a job –
'cold'. Rejecting an offer. Condolence. Letters of
reference. Congratulations. Letters of complaint.
Social letters. Summary.

4 Specialised Letters 63

Sales and appeals letters. Seeking donations. 'Hard sell' letters. Letters to Editors. Summary.

5 Good-Looking Letters 77

Opening and closing letters. Page layout. Stationery. Letterheads. Home-made letterheads. Business letterheads. Good typing (or handwriting). Letter length. Summary.

6 Good-Looking Reports 99

Report lengths. Report content and headings. Report layout. Illustrations. Production. Summary.

7 Other Writing Matters 113

Writing for the Press. Writing a manual. Word processing. The computer. Keyboards and monitors. Storage. Printers. The word processor Program. Electronic mail. Books about writing. Summary.

Appendix 133

Hints – for writing even more effective letters.

Index 135

INTRODUCTION

"Ah, there's the post. What have we got today?"
"I'd particularly like that letter to catch tonight's post please, Dianne."
"Look at all these lovely letters and cards the postman has brought you, Sally."

Despite today's near-universal availability of the telephone, the ordinary letter still retains all of its old importance. To some even, it is exciting. Who has not waited anxiously for a letter from a loved one, for the response to a job application, or for the answer to a query?

A phone call is, of course, instantaneous (or at least, it should be) but it is often usefully preceded by an introductory letter or followed up by a written confirmation. A letter can be referred to, as often as necessary. A phone call is always ephemeral.

You could say:

> A call on the phone may bring someone closer;
> but a letter's better, you can read it again – and again.

At work, communicating with other workers, or at home, dealing with everyday business and a busy social life, letters are still an essential part of living today.

We all need to write letters. Letters to friends, letters to firms, business letters, sales letters, letters of congratulation or condolence, letters of reference. . . . Every day there are letters to write. The more effective your letter writing skills, the greater your chances of success.

Your letters say a lot about you; your letters are your personal ambassadors. If they appear confused, unintelligent, or . . . yes, "down-market", then right or wrong, this is how the reader will think of you. At your first face-to-face meeting, you will have an uphill struggle to overcome and change that impression. On the other hand, a well-presented, thoughtful and business-like letter will create an image of a sound, thoughtful, business-like person. You are immediately one step ahead of the field. A well-written social letter can certainly help to cement a friendship, and will often help to overcome a geographical separation.

Consider the fate of a letter to a large commercial or government organisation. Action on an unattractive-looking, poorly written letter, difficult to understand – and perhaps hard to deal with – may be deferred in favour of a letter that *looks* better. A straightforward, attractive-looking letter stands most chance of achieving its objective, quickly.

A well-structured, well-presented letter will always be more effective than a poorly conceived, poorly set-out one. To achieve that effectiveness you need to work at your letter writing. There are skills to learn and techniques to use. They all need working at.

The effective letter

What then are the qualities and requirements of a really effective letter?

To be most effective, a letter must:

- be well structured – make its points logically and convincingly
- be well written – readily understood by the reader
- look good – be well set out and give the impression of "quality".

Before that though, there is a need for a letter to have something to say: a purpose. Even with a social letter to a friend, you need to have *something* to say: some wee bit of news (or gossip) or a re-expression of feelings. With other than social letters it is important to recognise when NOT to write a letter.

An elderly acquaintance of mine, who grew up with the idea that people should be thanked for any service they provide, is prone to reply to every letter. She thanks her solicitor for telling her that a matter is resolved; she thanks her bank for confirming a transaction. If everyone were like her, the *system* would be clogged up with thank-you letters.

So . . . before sitting down to write a letter, identify your purpose. This will usually be either to persuade the recipient to do something, or to inform him/her of something. To persuade or to inform. Keep your purpose in mind all the while you are writing, or planning to write; let your purpose influence how you put your message across.

If you really *need* to write; will think about structuring your letter to achieve your purpose; will write simply – as though you were talking to an interested friend; and will make your letters *look good;* then you will write *effective letters*.

Other writings

But at work, if not elsewhere, it is not just letters and internal memoranda that have to be written. You will often need to write other things, press releases, other PR material, reports – even user manuals.

The same basic principles apply to report and PR writing as to letter writing. You still need to be clear about the identity, understanding and needs of the reader; you still need to be clear about your own purpose; and you still need to structure the writing to best achieve that purpose. But the longer and more formal papers need a rather more formal approach. We will touch on the principles of writing other than letters – and point you in the direction of further advice.

Now, to work. First, the planning stage.

1

THE PLANNING STAGE

If you are to write a really effective letter, or any other document for that matter, the first thing to do is to plan it. You need to sit down and think about it.

At this stage, you need to think about:

- the recipient (the reader)
- the purpose of writing
- what you are going to write (the content)
- how best to put your point across (the structure).

Consideration of each of these points is part of the preliminary planning process of writing an effective letter. Lack of adequate consideration at this stage will mean a less than fully effective letter.

The reader

Perhaps the most important concept to grasp in the cause of more effective letter writing is the importance of the reader. "But that's obvious," you may say. "Of course one needs to think about the reader; that's who it is addressed to." Nevertheless, a lack of consideration of the reader's needs is one of the commonest of letter writing faults.

Writing to a child, it is almost second nature to simplify the expressions and words used. Writing to a professional colleague one often resorts to readily understood abbreviated technical jargon. At both these extremes the need for consideration for the reader is easily appreciated. In between, less so.

Think of sending Mum a postcard from a holiday hotel. You don't need to explain where you are, she knows; and even if she has forgotten, the picture on the front of the card should quickly remind her. She will have been waiting for the card to arrive (even though it may not come until after you yourself have returned), so you need no preamble. Its purpose is simply to reassure her that you have arrived safely and that she is not forgotten. Its content is almost taken for granted – you're enjoying yourself. You don't even need to sign it, Mum will recognise your writing.

All that's needed is something like:

> Mum / Arrived safely. Tracey sick on flight but OK now. Weather gorgeous, food passable, sea calm and drinks cheap. See you Friday. Love J + T.

Compare that with the sudden thought of sending a holiday card to a friend you haven't seen for ages. He will not immediately understand why someone – whose signature is perhaps indecipherable – should be sending him a saucy postcard from Katmandu. You need to explain much more.

You might perhaps say something like:

> Bill / Sorry we haven't seen you for ages. Jane's been sick

and I changed jobs. We're both recovering here in Nepal on a two-week camel-tour package. The camels are finding it heavy going but we're not. We're home on 23rd and will ring Monday to fix dinner-date. Jane + Tom.

Notice how the brief message brings Bill quickly up-to-date on the essentials, has a touch of lightweight holiday humour, and says something positive – we'll fix up a dinner.

Similarly with business letters. If you are in frequent correspondence with a close business colleague you can dispense with some of the formalities when writing to him/her.

You might be in a position to write something like:

Dear Charles

Great news! We got the contract for the new school.

Can you expedite delivery of the hinges and let me have a further five hundred? I'll get Lucy to let you have the formal order before the end of this week. Let's meet for a drink Wednesday lunchtime to celebrate.

Yours ever

William.

Because you and Charles are in frequent and friendly contact, this letter is very clear. And most important, you *knew* that it would be clear to Charles. But suppose that Charles, with whom you had been dealing for a long time, had just left the other firm and his replacement had not yet done business at all with you. In that situation a very different letter would be required. Something like:

Dear Mr Dickins

We have not yet had the pleasure of meeting but I hope shortly to rectify that. I had a lot of dealings with your predecessor. You will find, from your records, that we have an outstanding order with you for 400 4″ chromium-plated rising hinges, due for delivery next month. We have recently won a contract for a new school building and work has to start very urgently. I wonder therefore whether you could bring forward the delivery of the 400 hinges. We would like them by the end of this month – and earlier if at all possible.

We shall also require a further 500 hinges of the same pattern. On the understanding that you can maintain the same terms for supplying these, I enclose our official order form. Please telephone me if there are any snags.

Yours sincerely

William Greensleeves

Notice here how much more explanation has to be given. The reader, a new man to the job, would not know any of the background; some he doesn't need to know, but what he does need to know, he has to be told. A more formal letter is almost inevitably longer.

You have thought about the recipient of your letter; you have accepted the concept that the message you convey, and the way in which it is put across, has to vary with the reader. Keep thinking along these same lines for a little longer.

Is your letter going only to the first reader? Is Mum going to want to show your card to other members of the family, or mutual friends? Does it therefore need to be written rather more carefully? More important, and in real life quite likely, will friend Charles need to show your business letter to his boss perhaps, to get approval for the expedited delivery or the increased order?

Before (and while, *see* page 13) writing any letter –

or report or press release – think first, last, and all the time, about the reader (*See* Fig. 1.1); and then think again, about the possibility of there being a second reader. How much will that second reader be able to understand? You may need to adjust your writing style to accommodate the different needs of the likely second reader.

What You Need to Know . . .

                        . . . About Your Reader

- Knowledge: how much does the reader know about the specific subject of your letter?
- Education (not the same as specific knowledge): how much, and at what level, do you need to explain? *And* in what discipline is the reader educated? (A reader with, say, an MSc in engineering will require different aspects to be explained in different ways than a reader with, say, an MA in Norse mythology or an MBA. They will see things differently.)
- Native language and customs: if English, no problem; if other, you may need to allow for this when explaining.
- Motives: are the reader's motives financial or wholly altruistic; personal-prestige- or community-related? The reader's motives will influence how a case is presented, the order perhaps in which points are made.
- Authority: to what extent has the reader the authority to make the decisions you are seeking? (The answer will influence thoughts of a second reader.)
- Relationship: is the reader a relation or friend, and if the latter, how close?
- Identity: can you identify an individual reader, or must you merely address a large impersonal organisation?

FIG. 1.1

(An excellent example of this concept is when writing a letter to the editor of a newspaper. The editor may be the final arbiter on whether or not your letter is published, but he/she is certainly not the one for whom the letter is really intended. Your "Letter to the Editor" has to be written for, and is meant to be read by, the newspaper's readers.)

The purpose

Just as important as knowing your reader, you should know why you are writing: your *purpose*.

Once again, your response is likely to be, "That's daft. Of course I know why I'm writing. I'm writing to tell . . . about . . . ;" or, ". . . I'm writing to ask for. . . ." Sometimes that response is correct – but not always. Too often, a writer is insufficiently clear about the real *purpose* of a letter and, in consequence, the result is woolly and lacking in direction.

It is perfectly reasonable to define the purpose of any letter (or report or press release) as being either to inform the reader about something, or to persuade the reader to do something. But it is more helpful to expand this definition; and again we return to thoughts of the reader.

It is not enough for the letter to have an objective of persuading the reader to do something if it does not result in the reader being so persuaded. This is not *effective* letter writing; it is ineffective. We also need to define the result, the action, we are seeking.

The objective of writing a holiday postcard home to Mum is to inform her that all is well, you are having a good holiday . . . *and* to relieve any unspoken worries she may have about you, your safety, and her continued, unforgotten, importance. The objective in sending a postcard to old friend Bill is to mend the fences damaged by your previous failure to keep in contact. These objectives are achieved in the postcards. The purpose is clear; therefore so is the message.

Similarly, the purpose of each of the business letters is clear. To persuade Charles, or Mr Dickins, to expedite delivery and to increase the order (at the same price). And again, the objectives are met. There was also perhaps a hidden objective – to reassure the recipient that the letter-writer's business was doing well. But this reassurance is put over fairly delicately.

We can now therefore better define the likely purposes of a letter (or other similar document) as:

- to *inform* the reader of some necessary (ie relevant) facts – so that he/she can decide upon a course of action;
- to *persuade* the reader to take some action (not necessarily, but often, on the basis of factual information);
- to *establish, maintain or improve* a social or business relationship;
- to *create* a good impression of the writer in the mind of the reader.

And, as we have seen, a letter will often have more than one purpose. The primary purpose however, will almost always be one of the first two purposes listed above. The last two are – usually – secondary purposes.

When planning any letter or similar document, it helps to write down first, your primary purpose. Until you are happy with the effectiveness of your correspondence, do this for everything you write. Even when you are content with your abilities, you will still find it a helpful discipline for the more important documents.

The better you define your purpose, the clearer will the resultant document be.

Set down your purpose in the form: "To tell Mr Bloggs the different unit costs of 200, 400 or 1000 pairs of brass or chromium-plated hinges, so that he can decide the quantity and quality to order – from us."

Initially, you may also find it useful to remind yourself of the almost universal inevitable secondary purpose: "To maintain good relations with the reader and to convey a good impression of the writer." In time though, you will take these secondary purposes as read.

There may be occasions when you need to remind yourself of the secondary purpose though. I may, for instance, think of writing a stiff letter to an editor who has too long delayed a decision on, or a payment for, a feature article I have submitted *on spec*. My primary purpose is clear: "To persuade the editor to expedite a decision (or payment) – in my favour." But my secondary purposes in writing to an editor are always: "To maintain a good relationship with the editor (such that he/she will continue to look favourably on the work I submit to him/her); and to maintain a professional and business-like impression."

I have to think very carefully about such a letter. My primary purpose may conflict with my standard secondary purposes. If I write too "stroppy" a letter a busy editor may decide I am just a nuisance; reject my article and avoid future dealings. I may therefore decide to write only a very mild "chaser".

Alternatively, I may decide that I don't much care for this particular editor/magazine; that more than anything else, I want my article back or paid for; and that I can live with the consequences of possibly closing this market for my work. In that situation I can afford to write a strongly worded letter.

The important thing is that you should know what you are doing.

When you come to write the letter, you will have the purpose set down in front of you throughout. Everything you write will be directed to achieving that objective.

We also need to ask ourselves why we are proposing to write at all. Do you need to write that letter? Or are you writing just for the sake of writing? (We have all seen letters and internal business memoranda that have little point – except perhaps to keep the sender's name known. Which of course can itself be an acceptable purpose.) We can best answer questions as to whether or not we should be writing at all if we carefully define what we are to write about.

The content

Once more, some may think that the question of what you are going to write about is unnecessary. But think again of the reader.

Does the reader know the background to the subject? Does the reader *need* to know the background? Does the reader need to know *all* the facts – or may he/she find it easier to make the right decision without the peripheral information? (Take care though. Necessary information should, of course, never be withheld.) Will the reader understand what you are writing, or is some explanation required? On the other side of the same coin, will the reader feel that you are "teaching Grandma to suck eggs" if you explain unnecessarily?

You need to adjust the content of a letter, or any other document, to the needs of the reader.

For a while, until you gain confidence, make a practice of briefly listing the points to be made, the facts to be advised, the explanations that will be necessary, in every letter. This practice should always be followed in the more important, and longer, letters and reports.

And this is not just a counsel of perfection for business letters; it is equally appropriate for social letters too. (Have you never sealed down a letter and then realised that you have forgotten to mention something important?) It helps too, to ensure that you have something to say, a purpose, and are not writing for the sake of writing.

Having listed the necessary points, facts, etc., you can then decide which are the most important and, even at this stage, whether some can still be omitted. And you can arrange the content in the way most likely to achieve the purpose of the letter. This arranging of the order is the development of the structure of the letter.

The structure

Without a predetermined structure – which, as we shall see, for most letters need only be a simple unwritten one – your writing can appear vague and purposeless. It will lack direction; and will usually fail to achieve its purpose.

Consider an unstructured letter of complaint to, say, the Gas Board:

Dear Sirs,

I am sorry to have to write to you today, but I have just come back from a holiday in Greece. I tried telephoning you before I went, but could get no response. I have a feeling that gas is escaping from somewhere in my flat. When I went on holiday I was so worried about this that I turned off the gas supply at the mains. Now I am back though, I need the gas cooker on, but I am still scared to do this. I think the fault may be where I used to have a gas fire in the lounge until I sold it to the men from the Electricity Board who came to take my fridge away. They said they would tell you about the need to stop off the connection but perhaps they forgot. Certainly you didn't come. Please help me; I'm fed up with living on salads, cold meat and cold drinks. And I really do believe there is a gas leak.

Yours faithfully

Mabel Ashington (Miss)

Leaving aside the fact that a telephone call would have been a better way of dealing with this problem, Miss Ashington's letter is vague and unstructured. Its purpose is clear; it will probably have the desired effect; but it is very badly written.

Think how much more effective it would have been if it had said something more like:

Dear Sirs

I wish to report a probable gas leak at the above address. I have turned off the main gas supply but cannot continue without cooking facilities for long.

I believe the leak may have been caused by the recent removal of a gas fire by the Electricity Board workmen, who said that they would notify you of the need to seal off the pipe. This has not yet been done.

Can you please come quickly and deal with the gas leak. I am very concerned about the potential danger.

Yours faithfully

Mabel Washington (Miss)

Whereas the first letter was full of irrelevant information all jumbled up without semblance of logical order, the second letter is very clear and well-structured. The second letter opens with a clear statement of its purpose, then provides the essential facts, and finally makes quite clear what action is requested.

So, from that example, we have established perhaps the most useful structure for an "ordinary" business letter. It needs a beginning, a middle, and an end. Or, more specifically:

- an introduction – which may usefully incorporate a statement of the purpose of the letter;
- a statement of the *relevant* facts – plus any associated opinions (as long as it is made clear which are opinions and which are facts);
- a clear statement of what action is required.

This simple structure – a beginning, a middle and an end – is particularly appropriate for the sort of personal business letters that everyone has to write from time to time. It is equally appropriate to many letters of a more social nature. And it can be extended to meet the needs of formal business letters, internal memoranda and full-scale reports. (We will look at how it extends to the needs of full reports below.)

See how well it meets the requirements of a social letter inviting someone to dinner:

Dear Julie

Can you and Andrew come out to dinner with us next Friday week? We've got a visiting fireman over from Tom's firm's American subsidiary and we'd like him to meet some of our friends in the same line of business. We're also asking Mary and David, and the Simpkinsons – from Gemini Foods, in case you haven't met them.

We'll get together at 8 in the bar at The Golden Fleece, here in Muddlecombe, and we'll eat about 9. The food's always good there.

Give me a ring this week to confirm that you can come. Do say yes. I need your cheerfulness to see me through.

Yours

Jane

It works well:

- Introduction: the purpose – an invitation.
- Middle: the facts – who, what, where and when.
- Ending: the action – ring and accept – and a "deadline".

Now see how the same structure works with a simple everyday business letter:

Dear Mr Bloggs

Thank you for your letter of 29 February. You ask for more details of my mining experience.

I was employed for fifteen years (1960–75) by Guano Mining Incorporated, of Alaska, and worked exclusively in the Far East. In that period, I supervised the excavation of a total of approximately 15 million tons of guano from caves in Borneo, Indonesia and the Phillipines. Hand tools only were used throughout, and I became an acknowledged expert in re-sharpening the hoes which are the preferred local implements.

Should you wish further information, please telephone me. I now look forward to your approving my application to mine the Muddlecombe guano caves. I need your approval before the end of this month. If I cannot start then, the birds will be into the mating season and excavation will need to be delayed until next year. I know that neither you nor I want such a long delay.

Yours sincerely

Gabriel Goloshki

Again, the structure is effective:

- Introduction: purpose – response to identified request.
- Middle: facts – as requested, no more, no less.
- Ending: action – now please say yes, by a deadline.

Longer documents

In writing – or planning – any letter, and particularly the "middle" section, it is important to get the balance right. By this, I mean that you should not write too much on one aspect of a subject, and too little on another. You must ensure that points of roughly equal importance are treated with roughly equal respect – that is, at roughly equal length.

Balance is important with a one-page letter. It is even more important in a longer document.

The structure too of a longer document is of even more importance than the structure of a shorter letter. After all, it is not impossible to distil and mentally re-order the sense out of the first, jumbled, letter to the Gas Board. It would be far more difficult to make sense of a jumbled, direction-less, and poorly-structured 20-page technical report.

The structure of a longer letter or report is fundamentally the same as for a short letter. The essentials are, as always, a beginning, a middle and an end. But a report may have other elements. One simple standardised structure for a report is:

- Introduction – the reason for the report, how it relates to other reports, and the terms of reference (the purpose and how this was to be achieved);

- Background information – usually a statement of the problem (the first of the facts);

- Facts – including the source of the facts, and/or – briefly – the methods by which they were collected;

- Interpretation of the facts – still basically factual information;

- Conclusions and recommendations (for action) – well-founded but nevertheless inevitably subjective opinions derived from the interpretation of the facts;

- Summary – and it is arguable whether the summary should be placed at the end of the report or at the beginning. There is a good case – that some will want to read no more than just the summary – for the summary to begin the report. This has the advantage of facilitating the placing, very sensibly at the end, of . . .

- Appendices – details of technical processes, references, etc. which will be wanted by specialists, but not by "lay" readers.

There are other standardised structures for reports; they will all follow the same basic logic. That given above is particularly suitable, with such titular and subdivisional adjustments as may be necessary, for fairly lengthy technical reports. It is particularly important in any report to ensure that there is a clear differentiation between the facts (which are incontestable) and the recommendations (which are no more than the writer's views or judgement).

Where a report is relatively short – little more than a longish letter – an alternative approach is to pose questions of oneself and order these in a logical way to form the framework. Thus, for example:

- Why report? (Because the boss asked for a brief report.)
- Just what is this proposal on which I am reporting?
- What do I know (or can find out) about it? (Facts)
- Is it viable? (Opinion)
- What benefit for us will this proposal generate?
- Against that, what will it cost?
- How long will it take?
- What is the potential disadvantage in not proceeding?
- Do I recommend go-ahead?

And it is noticeable how even with this approach, the basic approach of introduction/purpose, facts and opinions, recommendation for action, is still relevant.

With suggested structures identified for the longer reports it is easier to appreciate the importance of ensuring balance. Too much writing about any one of the above elements, at the expense of one of the others, could bias the recommendation.

Word budgets

To ensure the right balance in a long document, there is merit in establishing, at the outset, a "word budget". This is not as difficult or traumatic as it sounds. It merely means that you should decide roughly the overall length of the complete document – and within that, how much space, or how many words, to allot to each topic.

The word budget need entail no more than listing the topics to be covered in a report and apportioning numbers of words to each topic. If you were engaged in, say, a small transport planning investigation, the word budget for the report might look something like:

Introduction: 250 words (half a close-typed page)
Terms of reference: 250 words (half page)
Definition of Problem: 250 words (half page)
Survey methods: 250 words (half page) per survey (2)
Data: One-page table per survey
Analysis/interpretation of data: 500 words (one page)
Two alternative solutions: 500 words (one page) each
Costed recommendation: 500 words (one page)
Summary: 250 words – but occupying a full page
Appendices: technical processes – as they come.

Such a pre-determined word budget would ensure that too much was not written about, for instance, the survey methods. A technical person would probably wish to expand on *how* they went about their work; a non-technical reader is more interested in the solutions which can be offered as a result of the study. The balance is geared to the needs of the reader.

A word budget becomes even more valuable with a major report. It is then possible that the writing of some sections of the report would be delegated to members of a team. In that situation, they need to be told how much to write – and held down to it.

Headings

A letter, and particularly a business letter, will often merit a title – it becomes a quick, "topic-identifying" part of the introduction. But apart from a title, many longer documents warrant further headings within the text. They are potentially very valuable as a means of the reader finding his/her way around the report; they break up the solid flow of text into manageable proportions. (They have other benefits too – *see* page 101.)

Headings need to be considered at the planning stage, in the context of the framework of a document. Often the topics to be covered will become the headings. But it is essential to decide on the *hierarchy* of headings before commencing writing.

It should almost always be possible to plan a report of up to, say, twenty pages, using no more than one "level" of heading. It should not be necessary to go into sub-headings. A very long, very complicated report might need headings and sub-headings but even then, good planning should be able to obviate this.

But the most important thing with a hierarchy of headings, once established, is that the hierarchy must be adhered to.

There can be few more confusing things than a long document wherein the heading style changes from, say, underlined lower-case typing to non-underlined capitals and then to underlined capitals. The reader does not know whether an item is a heading, a sub-heading within the previous section, or even a sub-sub-heading. The structure loses credibility. And the reader loses his/her way.

No matter how good the writing style (*See* next chapter), any letter or report can be ruined "at conception" by poor planning and – particularly reports – by the confusion of an illogical heading structure.

Summary

1 Effective letter writing depends on consideration of the reader, the purpose of the letter (including whether or not there is even a need to write at all), the content of the letter, and the structure. And the same principles apply equally to longer documents – business reports, etc.

2 To write effectively, the writer must write with the reader in mind. Different readers will have different needs, different interests; these must be considered. The good writer is one who thinks first and foremost of the needs of the reader.

3 There should always be a well-defined purpose in writing a letter. Never write just for the sake of writing. The main purposes are to inform the reader (to facilitate action), to persuade the reader (to act), to develop a good *rapport* with the reader, and to foster a good impression of the writer.

4 The points to be made in a letter should be listed, thought about, ranked in importance, and then brought together in a logical structure.

5 For a letter, the commonest – and probably the best – structure is: introduction (and purpose); factual

information; request for action. A beginning, a middle, and an end. The same basic structure, elaborated somewhat, is equally relevant to longer documents.

6 It is important to get the balance of a letter, or even more important, a longer document, right. For longer documents, this can be made easier by determining a word budget.

7 For long documents too, a hierarchy of headings should be established at the planning stage – and strictly adhered to.

2

WRITING STYLE

You've planned your letter: determined its purpose, its content and its structure; now you can begin to write. But wait: first, let's think a little more about our reader and our purpose.

Irrespective of any specific purpose which we have determined in the planning process, our underlying and fundamental purpose is to *communicate*. Our purpose in writing is to *communicate* our views, our information to the reader. Until the reader has received that information, those views, the communication process *has not happened*. If the reader is not able to understand the information we are seeking to impart, the communication process is again not completed.

In simpler terms, the process of communication requires an unimpeded flow, from sender (writer) to receiver (reader). Anything which impedes that flow hinders the communication process.

The most likely impedance to the flow of communication is the writer not thinking of the needs of the reader. Some writers seek to impress their reader(s) with their cleverness, by the way in which they can "turn a phrase". Such writers are selfish; they are thinking more of their needs than of those of the reader.

Transparent writing

The best writing style is that which is "transparent". Transparent writing goes unnoticed; the reader can occupy him/herself fully in absorbing the flow of information, views, comments, etc.

(When you read a "rattling good yarn", or a "good read", you seldom if ever notice the author's writing style; you are far too engrossed in the story to bother about the occasional blemishes in the writing style. In fact, the writing style of some of the better-selling story-tellers sometimes leaves a lot to be desired. But it doesn't matter. Their purpose was to get you, the reader, involved in the story; and this the good ones achieve magnificently. Their actual writing is transparent.)

How then can you learn to write transparently? There are a few rules of thumb, but before we come on to them, let us think more generally.

When you talk to a close friend about a common interest or hobby you probably speak with enthusiasm. Certainly, you will talk in an easy way, without inhibitions, and in a manner which both you and your friend easily understand. This is communication at its best. It is "transparent" talking; no-one notices nor cares if you drop the odd *H* or muddle the occasional tense. If you now try to explain the joy of your hobby to an interested but unaware potential recruit you will talk more simply, more understandably – but equally clearly. You know your subject. You will communicate well.

Now you must learn to write in much the same way as you spoke. One American management and communication guru, Robert Gunning, expresses this idea well, as he advises writers to "Write as you talk". (He doesn't mean that you should do the two things at once.) The concept might perhaps be better expressed as "Write the way you (would like to) talk" – that is, simply and clearly, and without the "ums" and "ers" and the grammatical slips.

Let's repeat that, and emphasise it, because it is an important "rule".

WRITE THE WAY YOU TALK

Writing simply

A major characteristic of *transparent* writing is its clarity – its clearness. Writing clearly entails writing in as simple a way as possible. If something is written clearly and simply it will be readily understood. Lack of understanding is one of the main barriers to communication.

Mark Twain was a great advocate – and exponent – of clear simple writing. He said it all, in a nutshell, in his advice to a writer:

> I notice that you use plain, simple language, short words and brief sentences. That is the way to write English. It is the modern way and the best way. Stick to it.

The clear, simple writing advocated by Mark Twain can best be achieved by following a few basic rules which expand on the above statement. These require that you write using:

- short words
- short sentences
- short paragraphs
- simple punctuation.

Short simple words

Short words first. Why short words? Basically because most people – readers – readily understand short words. And many people find long words difficult.

Consider this sentence:

> In 1746, according to Romilly, "such was the state which the inflammation of men's passions had attained", the Jacobite, Francis Towneley was executed "in the *plenitude* of those attending, disgusting barbarities which he had submitted to the *reprobation* of the House."[Paraphrased from E. S. Turner, *Roads to Ruin*, Michael Joseph, 1950]

Apart from the fact that I find the whole sentence very hard to understand anyway, (for which I take only limited responsibility, having done no more than slightly re-order the original) the two long words which I have shown in italics drove me quickly to the dictionary. (I chose this sentence solely for its long words – and because it was bound to be out of copyright.) And even after looking them up, I was but little wiser.

The words were written long ago and are of a legal nature, always a good source for difficult words. The real point though, is that I had to go to the dictionary to look up their meaning. My reading was interrupted; communication was broken. Many (most?) readers would not bother to consult the dictionary; they would skip the section, hoping it was not of great importance. If there were too many such sections most readers would just give up altogether.

(This example was extreme, the better to make the point. But less extreme examples certainly abound in everyday business letters, if not so often in social correspondence.)

If you will restrict yourself – as far as possible – in

your letter writing, to the use of short words, your readers will understand more of what you write. You will therefore retain their attention. Your letters will be more effective.

There was however, an important qualification in the advice in the previous paragraph. "As far as possible." Sometimes it will be essential to use a long word; it may be the *only* correct word. In such cases, use the long, unusual, difficult word – and then do your best to explain its meaning. (An explanation can sometimes be inferred from the way the word is used, but don't try this too often.)

But, in general, avoid long – "hard" – words, words of more than three syllables; avoid words not in everyday use by people of the intellect and education of your reader. Instead, use as many short, simple, everyday words as necessary to make the same point.

Short simple sentences

The next basic rule of clear, simple writing is to use short sentences. By short sentences I mean an average length of about 15 or 16 words, and a maximum of around 25. (And remember, to average out at 15, if just one sentence is 25 words long, there must be one at 5, or two at 10, and so on, to balance it.)

Why do I recommend using short sentences? Because short sentences are usually easier to understand. They make a single point, and they make it quickly. The reader doesn't need to think twice to see what the writer is aiming at.

That is not to condemn long sentences. There are many writers who write very well, and yet they consistently use long flowing sentences. But it requires considerable skill to write a long sentence well; less skill is needed to write a short sentence. And your object is to write letters – not literary masterpieces. So take the easy course, and write in short sentences.

Before leaving the subject of short sentences though, I should clarify the length measurement. For the purpose of this advice I treat as sentences, not merely the strings of words ending with a full stop (or question or exclamation mark), but also those closed with a colon or semi-colon. (Yes, I know. That sentence was 35 words long. But I couldn't make the point with fewer words. So I broke my "maximum" rule. But notice how I have successfully brought my average right back down, within this paragraph.) As we shall see later, an independent clause ending *correctly* with a semi-colon, could as easily be a sentence in its own right.

And I have just demonstrated another important point about writing style. The "rules" I am setting out here are not set on tablets of stone. They are guides, not laws. Break them if you wish: but do so knowingly and for good reason, not unintentionally.

Having taken on board the idea of short sentences though, you must still apply common sense to the concept. A letter with nothing but short, punchy, sentences would feel wrong. Short sentences suggest action, they generate urgency.

> He ran down the alleyway. The footsteps followed. Suddenly, a cat screeched from the top of a wall. Lights blazed on. A gun fired. He felt a sudden sharp pain. He was hit. But he still knew what was going on, so at least he wasn't dead.

Phew! I'm breathless. But I have, I think, made the point.

Similarly, long flowing sentences will tend to slow down the action.

> He walked, quietly and cautiously, along the darkened streets, glancing all the while, from side to side. He was looking for the entrance to the house where he had been taken the night before.

That seems to me to have far less sense of urgency than the short-sentence example.

In letter writing – and the writing of other documents too – you should vary the lengths of your sentences. Don't write all short sentences, nor all "average" length ones. And certainly not all long ones. Try to open and close each paragraph with a shorter than average sentence: make the initial point quickly and positively; end with a punchy comment. But of course, writing is not a mechanistic process; you will not always be able to work to such an ideal sequence. But do bear the thought in mind.

Short paragraphs

Short, simple words can be strung together into short, simple sentences. Sentences are grouped together in paragraphs. And, to make your letter writing more effective, paragraphs too should be kept short.

You are advised that words and sentences should be kept short so that they are easily understood. Paragraph lengths should also be kept short. But the reasons for this are more complex. A paragraph should contain *no more than* a single main point in an argument or exposition; but paragraph lengths also have an effect on the appearance of a page.

Decisions on paragraph lengths are therefore a matter of considering both content and appearance.

First, the content. A fresh paragraph signals to the reader that he/she is probably moving onto a fresh stage in the discussion. He/she prepares mentally for this step. If the writer introduces a fresh topic in mid-paragraph, the reader will not be so prepared. The writing itself will have come between the writer and the reader, and interrupted the flow of ideas.

A writer can sub-divide a long single-topic paragraph without distracting the reader but should never introduce a second (or third) topic within a paragraph. And when a writer splits a single-topic paragraph into two it is helpful to make the link clear in the writing.

(I had to think for quite a while, myself, about the previous two paragraphs. Should they be all in one – from "First, the content." through to ". . . clear in the writing."? The second follows logically on but introduces a new facet of the topic. I played safe and split them. That could not be wrong; to leave them as one, might have been.)

The length of a paragraph has a considerable effect on the appearance of a page. We shall see, in Chapter 5, the importance of the layout of letters and other written work. For now, consider how each fresh paragraph gives an impression of relief in an otherwise overall greyness of continuous print. This relief comes from the blank spaces at the starting indent (often now omitted) and at the stopping short of the paragraph end. The blank space helps to lighten up the page appearance. In most letters, both typed and hand-written, even more space is created by the blank line which is now usually left between paragraphs. (Again, *see* Chapter 5.)

Long paragraphs provide few "beginning-and-end" blank spaces; short paragraphs provide many. But the frequency of these spaces also depends on the *width* of the column of writing. When writing a letter to a newspaper editor, or for a report to be printed with several columns on a page, the paragraph lengths will need to be much shorter than those appropriate to a typed document.

Having clarified the reasons, let us suggest suitable paragraph-lengths for letters. And these will be appropriate for "normal" letters and reports, not for those to be printed in narrow columns.

A useful average paragraph length to aim at would be around 60 to 80 words; an absolute maximum length should be around 150 words. In terms of numbers of sentences, these suggestions could be interpreted as around four or five sentences in an average paragraph – and never more than about seven or eight. Once again though, as with sentence lengths, it is important to vary the pattern. Use some short paragraphs and some longer ones. Don't make them all "too much of a muchness".

Simple punctuation

It has been difficult to reach this stage in the discussion about writing style without mentioning punctuation. Indeed, I have not succeeded. The earlier reference to the role of the semi-colon was unavoidable. And really, every reference to short sentences is itself a recommendation for simple punctuation.

A short sentence seldom needs more punctuation than a full stop at the end; but a comma will often ease the understanding of the sentence, and is therefore added. You will not go wrong if you restrict your punctuation to no more than full stops (and question marks) and commas. Remember that the only purpose of punctuation is to ease the reader's understanding, to improve the communication process. If you think a comma will make your sentence easier to understand – and if you can't serve the same purpose by improving your choice of words – then insert a comma.

It is usually only in longer sentences that a writer might feel the need for "more sophisticated" punctuation. But we have already advised against longer sentences anyway. So, as a general rule, stick to full stops and commas only.

Relax that rule if you need to introduce a list of items. Lists should always be prefaced with a colon – which does not need, and should not be given, an accompanying dash – and each item should perhaps be "closed" with a semi-colon. (If the items in the list are individually brief though, it is unlikely that semi-colons are required at all. *See* the list earlier in this chapter, page 27, wherein other than at the last line, I have left individual listed items unpunctuated.)

As we have already discussed, a semi-colon should be used to close an independent clause which is nevertheless closely related to a following – equally independent – clause. A good test of when to use a semi-colon is to check whether it could be replaced by a full stop. Both parts of a sentence divided by a semi-colon must be complete in themselves.

Use of the exclamation mark should be avoided almost entirely. (I have used one in this chapter. It is, I believe, alone in the whole book.) An exclamation mark is generally an admission of defeat, of inability to emphasise a point without it. It is the mark of an amateur.

So too is underlining. Underlining is not truly punctuation, but where else can we discuss it? Underlining should very seldom be necessary to emphasise a point; sufficient emphasis can almost always be achieved by the use of words alone. (When writing for publication – a "Letter to the Editor" perhaps – underlining will always be typeset as italic script, which is not particularly emphatic.)

The use of parentheses is a matter for some debate. "Literary" writers will usually avoid using phrases in brackets; technical writers do it often. Letter-writers can, I suppose, use brackets, but in moderation. Use them where they improve the "understandability". (A long coined word, pardonable only because it is really two shorter words joined together.)

Much the same advice applies to the use of the dash. The dash is considered, by purists, to be a lazy person's alternative to correct punctuation. It is often used instead of a bracket or a comma. I am prone to use the dash rather a lot – but I try to control myself. I like pairs of dashes, because they seem to draw more attention to their "contents" than do pairs of brackets or the comma.

Use dashes sparingly; use a pair as eye-catching parentheses; or use one on its own when you want to end a sentence with a twist, as I did in the previous paragraph.

One other punctuation form that is worth commenting on is the ellipsis – "dots" to you. Dots should not be used as an alternative to a dash. Dots have a specific role, to indicate the omission of words; as such, the three dots are a useful writer's tool. Use dots when you don't wish or need to complete a well-known quotation ("Money is the root . . ."); where there may be more to say, but you don't want to say it ("But . . ."); or where you are quoting only part of a sentence, statement or document ("That this nation, under God . . . shall not perish from the earth." *Abraham Lincoln, The Gettysburg Address*.)

Technical points. The ellipsis (dots) should consist of three dots – not four, nor five, and not asterisks – preceded and followed by a normal space. If at the end of a sentence, the ellipsis should not be followed by a full stop.

Writing tone

Having explored the relatively "hard" stylistic rules or guidelines, let us now consider "tone". Writing can be straightforward and down-to-earth, or it can be pompous and patronising. But if you *write the way you talk* this should ensure that your writing is easy and readable.

But there is further advice that can be offered, which is most usefully given in the form of a list of short suggestions:

- Prefer *active* rather than *passive* statements. An active statement might, for instance, be: "Sheila has checked our hotel reservations." The same statement, in passive form, might be: "The hotel reservations have been checked by Sheila." (Note that the passive approach is usually longer than the active.)

- Avoid written "pauses for thought" – the literary equivalent of the spoken "ers" and "ums" – such as "It should be noted that . . ." or "As has been said, . . ."

- Avoid Latin (Latin particularly, but other foreign words too, unless essential) jargon, slang and initialised titles that are not universally well-known. (UNO is acceptable, an internal office abbreviation is not.) If you are thinking about the reader, this piece of advice becomes redundant.

- Seek to be positive in your statements, without more use of "possibly" and "perhaps" than can be helped.

- Take care to avoid using tautological statements such as "He sat alone, by himself."

- Remember that the ultimate cannot be qualified: you cannot be slightly pregnant or very unique or even absolutely excellent.

- Avoid exaggeration, which can be construed as inaccuracy, and once identified, tends to weaken rather than strengthen an argument.

- Occasionally, ask a rhetorical question and then answer it. This generates a certain impact. I have used this form a few times in this chapter.

- Avoid writing in any way that can possibly be construed as dictatorial, grudging, indifferent, patronising, self-important, impertinent, racist or sexist. (You will have noticed my use of "he/she" throughout this book. I was once taken to task by a reader of another of my books for implying that secretaries were inevitably female. I have, I hope, learnt my lesson.)

- Do not, as an automatic reaction based on childhood schooling, avoid starting sentences with "And" or "But". The teachers were wrong. The Bible does it, Shakespeare does it, and so does Dickens. To start a sentence with "And" or "But" – in the right circumstances – creates a lot of impact.

- Avoid excess use of capital letters. It is better to err on the side of cautious non-use than to over-sprinkle your writing with incorrectly used capital letters. Use capitals for the start of a sentence and for proper names – and for little else. And, like underlining, the use of capitalised words for emphasis suggests that you cannot generate this emphasis through your writing alone.

- Exercise great care in the use of such qualifying words as *very* and *really*. *Very* and the word it qualifies can usually be replaced by a more appropriate single adjective. *Really* is usually unnecessary; it is often a last-ditch attempt to add colour to an otherwise flat statement. (But you will notice that I use both words on occasions.)

- Avoid the use of cliché-like groups of words which circle around the intended meaning. (*See* Fig. 2.1.)

What You Need to Know . . .

                . . . About Avoiding Circumlocution

Words and phrases to avoid	*Preferred alternatives*
with the minimum of delay	quickly
with the result that	so that
in the event that	should
valued at	worth
take action on	act on
in short supply	scarce
the way in which	how
make allowances (for)	allow (for)
it is my understanding	I understand
it has been stated herein	as stated
it should be added (*or* . . . noted)	furthermore (*or* note)
it is apparent that	apparently
in the field of (engineering)	in (engineering)
in the direction of	towards
clearly	–
it is clear that	–
in fact,	–
make an application	apply
enclosed please find	I enclose
despite the fact that	although
take into consideration	consider
during the course of	during
reduce to a minimum	minimise
of a permanent nature	permanent
constitutes	is
consists of	is
for the purpose of	for (*or*, to)

Actual writing

At last, having heard all the basic rules and all the advice about "tone" and "writing style", you are ready to start the actual writing. From your planning, you know what you are going to say, and now you know how you are going to say it.

Do not, however, think that what you now write will be the finished letter (or report). Far better to think of it as the draft. There are two reasons for this attitude: firstly, that it will not immediately be as good as it can be (good letters are not just written – they are *rewritten*); secondly, because if you recognise that it is *only a draft* you are less likely to get worried – and stuck.

Start the draft of your letter with the firm intention of completing it within a single page of typescript if at all possible. (Say 3–500 words if in handwriting.) Remember the standard letter structure: introduction (and purpose); facts; action required. Off you go.

If you are drafting in handwriting, I recommend that you write initially on alternative lines of lined paper. The blank lines leave room for you to correct and amend; you will need this room.

Once you have finished the long-hand draft you can begin to improve it. You have something on which to work.

Polishing

Go through your first draft and count the words in each sentence. Have you gone over the 25-word limit anywhere? If so, look carefully at the offending sentence: is there an "and" somewhere in the middle that can be replaced by a full stop? Are there long, woolly phrases – in the long sentence or anywhere else – that would be better omitted, or replaced with a single, crisper, word? Can you simply rewrite the offending sentence in a different and shorter way?

Add together the sentence lengths in each paragraph. Have you made one of the paragraphs too long? Maybe you can make it into two linked paragraphs. Read each paragraph carefully and in turn, to check that the content is internally consistent and homogeneous. If not, you need to split the offending paragraph to preserve the single-mindedness of its parts.

Now read the whole draft *aloud*. You want to *hear* your words coming back through your ears. Merely reading to yourself is not enough; that way, only "the eyes have it".

We are all prone to write the odd pompous phrase. Reading aloud will help you to identify such phrases – and cut them out. Reading aloud will also serve as a useful check on the effectiveness of your punctuation – so long as you pause only at punctuation marks.

While reading aloud, watch out too for the "well-turned phrase", the piece of "beautiful writing". Identify it; cross it out; then write it again, more simply.

Finally, make sure that you have included all the points you wanted to make; make sure that the logic of the sequence is still there; put yourself in the position of the reader, and make sure that all you have said is clear; and make sure that you have done the best you can to achieve your purpose.

Now, you can write out your letter as a "fair copy", or have it typed, or run if off on good quality paper on the word processor.

Other checks

You may well read about ways of checking the readability of written work. There are formulae and there are indices; there are even computer programs that will do such checks for you, as you write.

The best known index of readability is Robert Gunning's Fog Index. (Robert Gunning of "Write as you talk" fame.) To determine this index you have to count the words in each sentence, count the number of "hard" words (root words of over three syllables) and perform a careful, and quite involved, calculation; the result of this supposedly equates to the reading age necessary to understand the writing. The Fog Index is a good technique. But the advisory "rules" which I have outlined above, about lengths of words, sentences and paragraphs, will ensure a good Fog Index value – without the need for calculation.

In the next chapters we will look at examples of several specific types of letter, before moving on to the way in which a letter (or other such document) is best presented.

Summary

1 The best writing style is that which is "transparent", writing which does not impede the communication of ideas.

2 A basic rule for good, clear, transparent writing is to *write the way you talk*.

3 Simple, clear writing springs from:

- short (easy) words
- short, but varying length, sentences (15 words average, 25 words maximum)
- short, but varying length, single-topic, paragraphs (60–80 words average, 150 words maximum)
- simple punctuation (mainly full stops and commas).

4 While writing, think of the needs of the reader, and avoid the use of words or phrases which he/she would not understand or would be offended by.

5 Avoid waffling and over-writing. *Aim* to get a letter onto a single typed sheet of A4 paper, and the equivalent (3–500 words) if handwritten.

6 Draft first. Then check for sentence and paragraph lengths, for waffle, and for pomposities. Read aloud. Then rewrite: this is the polishing stage. A good letter is seldom just written, it is more usually rewritten.

3

EVERYDAY LETTERS

Before looking at the most important matter of presentation, the appearance of letters, it will help if we work on a few specific examples.

With which letters do most people have difficulty? Which letters do they wish to be most effective? The answer to both questions is probably the same – but will differ from person to person. Let us list some of the various types of letter. (And the order can only be random because different people's preferences will vary.)

There are:

- letters seeking help or information;
- letters seeking work – either seeking employment or selling one's services;
- letters rejecting someone else's offer of services to you;
- letters of condolence – on a bereavement;
- letters of reference – for friends or for colleagues changing jobs (not necessarily the same approach);
- letters congratulating a friend or colleague on a social, academic, or business achievement;

- letters of complaint – from the writer as individual or on behalf of his/her employer, about goods or services;
- purely social letters – gossip, invitations, love-letters;
- sales letters – on behalf of the firm – and charity appeal letters, which are much the same in principle;
- Letters to the Editor (of a magazine or newspaper);

There are inevitably other types of letter which cause some people problems but most other letters are relatively simple.

Now let us look at how we might write some of the letters listed above. And throughout, I shall endeavour to demonstrate how useful and relevant is the standard letter structure outlined in Chapter 1.

Seeking help or information

Letters seeking help or information are among the commonest types of letter in many organisations and businesses. When I am researching a new book I have to write such letters. If I describe what I do, this may help others with similar letters.

The first thing is to introduce myself and explain why I need information; then I explain just what I want, keeping the request as short and simple as I can; finally, I suggest how urgent the matter is – to me. Then I sit back and hope.

For this book, I wanted advice from busy newspaper editors on how they like their "Letters to The Editor". I wrote the following letter – which was effective in that it generated the replies that appear later:

Dear Mr Bloggs

I have been commissioned by my publishers, Allison & Busby, at W H Allen, to write a "How To" book on effective letter writing. The book will contain a section about writing Letters to the Editor of a newspaper. And I would like to include some comments from editors.

My purpose in writing to you is two-fold. First to ask if you have any advice to offer a budding letter-writer on how to write the sort of letter likely to be accepted. I shall make all the usual points about writing style, getting to the point quickly, and keeping the letter short; but I wondered if you could give me a few words of additional advice which I could quote.

My second purpose is to ask if you have any examples of "silly" letter submissions or amusing anecdotes that I could quote. I would like to include a little such light relief – how not to impress an editor.

I hope you will forgive me for imposing on you in this way. I realise you are busy, but a few moments of your time now might improve the quality of future "Letters". I enclose a stamped addressed envelope for your reply. I would much appreciate an early response. Thank you.

Yours sincerely

The framework worked fine there. I had to introduce myself first: the addressee didn't need a potted biography of me, all that was needed was to introduce myself *in this context*. The important point was that I was writing a book – and that I had a reputable publisher for it. (And by throwing in the possessive "my publishers", I hinted (truthfully) that I had worked with them before; that I was an established author.)

Next, I outlined my purpose: I wanted some help. In the next two paragraphs I expanded on this, explaining just what I wanted. I *called* my second and third paragraphs an outline of my purpose but in practice they were factual requests. And I also carefully made the point that I wanted *quotable* comments. If they replied, which most did, they knew full well that I was going to quote what they said, in this book.

Finally, I grovelled a little. I was after help, something for nothing, so I apologised, and tried to suggest that there might be some benefit for the editor. And I suggested – more in hope than in expectation – that there was some urgency in responding. I got several replies. But some took over a month to arrive. Generally though, it was an effective letter.

Selling yourself

Another type of letter now, selling oneself as a future employee or as a provider of a service. First, I can quote a letter which I wrote to a local Adult Education Office offering to run a one-day Saturday lecture course for them. This is what I wrote. Once again the standard letter framework *works*.

Dear Sir

CONTINUING EDUCATION PROGRAMME 19– –

I have seen your Spring 19– – programme of Activity and Skills Course and wonder if you might be interested in offering one-day Saturday courses in the next season. You are probably working on the programme for that season now. Your Spring programme is much geared to practical activities – and this is what I can offer.

I have run one-day courses . . . [and I briefly outlined my experience in running similar courses locally.]

I enclose a sheet outlining the one-day courses I can offer this year. Should you be interested I am sure we could agree a date to put on one of these. Let me also draw your attention . . . [Then I mentioned my fee and other conditions.] I look forward to hearing from you.

Yours faithfully

This letter was certainly effective in that I was asked to run two courses. And it conforms to the recommended framework. I think though, with hindsight, that I might have written it a little better.

It would have come to the point more quickly if, immediately after the first sentence, I had said, perhaps in a fresh paragraph:

> If so, I can offer two well-proven one-day courses: one on Writing Magazine Articles, and the other on How to Give a Talk. Both courses have already been successfully put on in Muddlesex. I attach details of the content of each course.

I could then have gone straight to the final paragraph, but starting with "Should you be interested . . ."

The resultant letter would have been shorter – therefore better – and more pointed. Notice too how I would have avoided the immediate necessity of the reader looking at the attachment, by giving the course titles in the body of the letter. Hindsight is a wondrous thing.

For another, rather more positive, type of "self-selling" letter, *see* Chapter 4.

Responding to job advertisements

Let us now look at a letter seeking employment. And as I have worked for the same employer for the last twenty years, I cannot here give a personal example. But I can advise from the "receiving end": I worked for many years as a personnel manager and dealt with a lot of internal promotion and recruitment. Job-seeking letters are very important; they need much care.

There are two types of job-seeking letter. By far the most usual is one in response to an advertisement, but jobs can also be sought "cold". We will look at both types. First the "response" letter.

Here is an invented, but likely-to-be-effective job application, based on sight of many originals:

Dear Ms Blacksock

TEAM LEADER (RESEARCH)

In response to your advertisement in the current issue of SCIENCE TOMORROW, I ask that I be considered for the post of Team Leader (Research) in your organisation (Post 632/92). As required, I enclose a copy of my CV; I also enclose a copy of my Skills Profile, which demonstrates how well my experience fits your needs.

I particularly invite your attention to my experience in leading a multi-disciplinary team of experts. With my present employer I lead a team of two graduate chemists, a chartered civil engineer and an economist. We have just finished developing a commercial process for building temporary bridges – of ice. I can tell you of this because the official launch of the process is next week. I am now looking for a fresh field to conquer.

I am available for interview at any time during the period you specify except on Tuesday 29 February – when I am presenting a paper on the Ice Bridge process to the Royal Society of Chemists.

I look forward to hearing from you.

Yours sincerely

There are several points to note in this letter. The recommended letter framework is again relevant. The title and the introduction make the purpose clear, and helpfully cite the appropriate references; it also mentions how the specified documentation has been amplified (by adding a useful Skills Profile); the bulk of the facts are in the attachments, but the letter is improved by picking out one selling point to emphasise; the action is up to the recipient, but the writer uses his one-day unavailability to make the point that he is giving a paper to a prestigious professional institution.

Notice too, how the letter is addressed to an individual by name. Often today, the advertisement gives the name of the person dealing with the recruitment. If not, it will pay to telephone the organisation and ask for a name. A personalised letter will always create a better effect than an impersonal, "Dear Sirs" one.

Often, not enough attention is paid – by the recruiting organisation – to the content of covering letters such as this; the bulk of the information is expected to be in the attached documentation. But if, by your letter, you can spark off even a little extra interest in the person sifting through the applications, it may get you one small step ahead of the opposition. A covering letter is well worth working on. A simple, "Herewith my CV. I look forward to hearing from you," just will not do.

Seeking a job – "cold"

Now, applying "cold" – without an advertisement on which to "hang" your bid. Most "cold" application letters go straight onto the "File and forget" file. (Or even worse, the "round file", the waste paper basket.) That is a fact of life. To be effective here, your letter must quickly make a major impact. It has to hit the spot – the right spot – immediately.

(I have heard of one job-seeking letter, that came in a takeaway-pizza-like box and was printed on a triangular slice of card. This was for a post in an advertising agency. Even in that gimmick-ridden field, I doubt whether such an approach would succeed. But at least it was novel – and it did get noticed.)

How then can we go about writing a "cold" job-seeking letter?

Think about the standard letter framework. The first thing is an introduction. Think positive. How can you start off your letter? You want to find some way of interesting the reader. Do you know anyone who works for the "target firm" whose name you can mention – or, better, to whom you can write direct? Or perhaps you have a contact – a college lecturer perhaps – who knows someone in the firm? The introduction to a "cold" letter is one of those spots where the "old boy network" helps a lot. It also helps to keep up-to-date with the trade news.

One of the following openings might be appropriate:

Dear Mr Smith

You may recall that we met at "Dental Quorum 88": I spoke in support of the paper you presented and we met afterwards, in the bar. Forgive my imposing on this brief acquaintance, but I believe that my experience and qualifications would be an asset to your organisation. And I got the impression that you were expanding your operations.

I have . . . [briefly outline relevant experience]

* * *

Dear Dr Doolittle

Dr Mary Wilberforce, my MSc tutor at Muddlecombe Polytechnic, tells me that she has spoken to you about me. I understand that you are considering setting up an internal training programme in Pictorial Mathematics for your staff; I believe that I would be the ideal person to introduce such a programme.

I have lectured for some years in conventional Mathematics and have recently been studying – in my own time – the important recent developments in pictorial presentation. There are very few experienced lecturers with an industrial background – as I have – and with knowledge of the new developments in this area.

I attach details of [basically a CV etc]

* * *

Dear Sir William

I notice, from a news item in yesterday's *Daily Bugle*, that Gemini Footwear are buying a controlling interest in the Czechoslovak firm LAVA Shoes. While I assume that you will retain many of the present management staff, it occurs to me that you might need a British presence to represent your interests.

I have fifteen years of experience in the British footwear industry – initially on the sales side, with Harvey Freeboot, and recently with The English Boot & Shoe Company as Senior Personnel Manager – and I speak fluent Czech. I also have considerable experience of working in Czechoslovakia; I was seconded there, from English BSC, for two years and actually worked in the LAVA offices. Czech labour relations are a minefield to the unititiated; and I have many useful contacts in their union movement.

May I call on you and expand on why I believe you need someone like me, urgently, in Prague? I will telephone your secretary on Thursday morning in the hope that I can arrange to meet you early next week.

* * *

The first example above, addressed to Mr Smith, uses a personal contact. (It is often worth keeping a record of useful people you meet; you never know when it may be important to know someone.) Notice how quickly the writer gets past the quick, "remember me" approach and on to the real business. And, to be really Machiavellian, it doesn't matter if the other person made no mention of any expansion. He/she will almost certainly not remember the conversation in detail – and it gives you the "entry" you need.

The second example links the introduction to a prior contact by a mutual acquaintance, the tutor. (You will have to push the contact to approach the potential employer.) And once again, notice how quickly the letter gets round to the point: "You need me". In this context, this is the first "factual" content of the letter; you then give just a few more facts explaining why.

In the third example, Sir William does not know anything about the writer. But he may well be impressed – if the writer is quick – by his/her initiative in seizing upon the news story.

The introduction shows the writer has initiative; the next item, the "facts", give a very brief explanation of why Gemini Footwear will need the writer's services, highlighting his/her particular skills; and the "action" part is very positive, the writer is going to act. Sir William cannot stop him ringing and may well agree to a short interview. (There is though, a danger that Sir William may think the final arrangements a shade too "pushy". You must make your own judgement on how positive to be in such circumstances.)

To repeat though, a "cold" job-seeking approach is always a gamble: an interview, or "file and forget", with the odds loaded against you. You may need to write several such letters to get a single interview. I do not know whether my example letters would succeed – but at least each one is a good try.

Rejecting an offer

Too frequently, you will get no reply at all, to many of your letters seeking employment. And not all letters in which you offer your services "for sale" will attract a response either. But we should always "do unto others . . ."; so let us consider how best to say, "No, thank you."

(As an author, I find that book publishers are often remarkably kind and helpful in their rejection letters; magazine editors however, perhaps because they receive more unsolicited material, seldom send more than a printed rejection slip.)

As before, the standard letter framework applies. The person to whom you are replying may well have despatched many letters; you should make it clear which one was "yours". Then you must give the fact – "no thanks" – plus anything else which might be helpful. There is no action to be taken, so you can probably stop such a letter off at this point. But some rejections offer helpful suggestions of what or where to try next; this is a pleasant way to round it off.

Dear Miss Witherspoon

Thank you for your letter of 25 December offering a variety of personal shopping services. As yet I do not need to avail myself of your offer; I am only in my forties and am quite capable of doing my own shopping.

However, I believe that your idea of offering to do the "heavy" shopping for older ladies living on their own is an excellent one, and I wish you every success. One of my neighbours, Mrs Dithers, may well find your service of occasional use; I have passed your letter to her. I believe she may be getting in touch with you.

Yours sincerely

That seems to me to be a very pleasant and helpful rejection letter; and even if nothing comes of it, the bitter pill of rejection has been sweetened. Notice though that the real meat of the letter, the "no thanks", is dealt with quickly and firmly. If you are not coldly positive in such rejections you invite a follow-up response to which you have to waste time writing a further letter to say "no" yet again.

If you were writing such a letter of rejection from your work-place you would say much the same thing – but probably less helpfully:

Dear Mr Sidcup

The Director has asked me to thank you for your offer of "back-up secretarial services" and to say that we see no need of such assistance in the near future. We are, however, keeping your address on the file and will be in touch should the need arise.

Yours sincerely

This one is sensibly brief; it is a slight put-down in that it is not from the person originally addressed; it is a clear rejection; and a wee bit of hope (which means very little) is offered in the final sentence. Mr Sidcup is lucky even to get a reply.

Condolence

Outside of the world of everyday business, there is one type of letter which regrettably we all have to write on occasions. This is the condolence letter. It may be a friend or relation who dies, or an employee; whoever it is, the letter to the surviving family is always a hard one to write.

A letter of condolence is one area where the standard framework falls down. All that you have to do is say how much you sympathise and how much you, and others, will miss the deceased. You need no introduction, there are no (new) facts, and no action is usually needed.

Most letters of condolence can be written along the lines of one of the following:

Dear Mrs Preast

I am writing to offer the sympathy of all Fred's friends and colleagues here at the factory, to you and your daughter on this sad occasion. Fred's death came as a very real and sudden shock to us all. The paint-shed will not seem the same without him. If there is anything that Stowell-Browns, or myself personally, can do to help you, please do not hesitate to let me know.

Yours sincerely

* * *

Dear Mrs Jones

I was very sad to hear the news about your husband. May I offer you sincere sympathies, both from myself and from the Bank in your bereavement.

Words are inadequate at such difficult times but I know that all your late husband's friends and colleagues would wish to be associated with this letter. He will be sadly missed by us all.

Yours sincerely

* * *

Dear Jean

No letter can help much at this sad moment but I wanted you to know how very sorry we both are. Henry was more than just a good friend; he was always so reliable, so happy, so utterly dependable. It seems impossible that we shall never again all laugh with him over the dinner table. We shall miss him a lot. If there is anything either of us can do – anything at all – do let us know.

With much love and all our sympathy,

Mary and Tom

Letters of reference

On a more cheerful note, let's return to the world of job-seeking. For every job-seeking letter that leads to an interview, there will be a call for "references". Many people find these hard to write. It is probably hardest to write about a friend, but it is not easy even to write about someone who works for you.

The standard letter framework works here, but only in part: the introduction – to establish to whom you are referring – is particularly important; so too is what you actually say about your friend or colleague; but there is no need to mention future action, which will be out of your hands.

There are four points to bear in mind when composing a reference:

- you must be completely honest in everything you say;
- you must ensure that you do not say anything that could be construed as libellous;
- you do not need to mention anything irrelevant to the position being sought;
- recruiting agencies are expert at reading between the lines of references.

A sample letter of reference might be along the following lines:

Dear Sir

Thank you for your letter of 17 June 19– –, seeking a reference for my friend James Duglets.

James and I have been close friends for about seven years now; I have also worked with him as a fellow salesman. To my certain knowledge James is a very good salesman; he frequently beat me to the monthly "top sales" bonus when we were together, some three years ago, at Slim-waist Ltd.

Outside of work, James is a solid family man and is much involved in community activities. I know he is a stalwart committee member of the local Parent-Teacher Association, and I believe he is also well thought of in the local Debating Society.

I am sure that he would be an asset on the Sales side of your organisation.

Yours faithfully

Notice how the full name and the relationship are made clear right at the start. Notice too how factual information is given where it was possible (James was the top salesman and is on the committee) and how the reference ends with a positive recommendation.

Had the reference been for a member of your staff it would have been rather different:

Dear Sir

JAMES DUGLETS

In your letter, Reference TH/658/91, dated 23 January, you ask for a reference for Mr James Duglets.

Mr James Duglets was employed by Slim-waist Ltd as a salesman from 27 March 19– – to 4 August 19– –. He resigned to take up a position with another firm closer to his home town. During this period of his employment with Slim-waist Ltd his performance was very satisfactory: he was on several occasions our "Salesman of the Month" and we were sorry to see him go.

During his employment with Slim-waist Ltd., his health and attendance record were both satisfactory.

Yours faithfully

Notice the rather more formal and factual approach to a firm's reference. The end ("SoM") part of the second paragraph was a bonus; many firms would not be so forthcoming. But notice again how well the whole letter conforms with the framework.

Congratulations

Letters of congratulation are straightforward. Follow the framework: say why you are writing and then give the fact – how pleased you are. They will be something like one of the following examples:

Dear Mr Bloggs

Thank you for telling me of your acceptance as a Member of the Institute of Stargazers. I know that this is a qualification towards which you have been working for several years and it has taken a lot of your spare time.

It is a prestigious qualification and I am very pleased for you. Please accept my sincere congratulations.

Yours sincerely

* * *

Dear Mary

What a lovely surprise! Ron and I had realised for some weeks that you and David were becoming close friends but we had not realised quite how attached you were becoming. I am so delighted; I am sure that you will make a fine couple. Do come over – both of you – and see us soon.

All our love

The first letter is formal – and obviously uses the framework; the second is just "straight from the heart" – the framework is there, but well submerged.

Letters of complaint

Another type of letter that is troublesome to many is that complaining of poor service or poor quality goods.

Perhaps the first thing to do when you are all "steamed up' and about to write a stiff letter of complaint is – to wait. Wait until you have cooled down. A letter written in the heat of the moment may turn out a bad letter; and it may land you in trouble for saying something rash. The best approach to a letter of complaint is a coldly precise one.

Refer back to the previous chapter. List the points that you wish to make to the defaulting organisation – and then check that you've got them right. Did they actually say that they would come on Friday? Did you make it clear that you wanted a blue chair and not a green one? Did their invoice have some small print about delivery charges – which you didn't notice?

A successful complaint is one in which you have all your facts right and the defaulter has no excuse.

You must also get the tone of the letter right. Initially at least, write a polite letter, asking for a correction of the fault and compensation if appropriate. If the recipient is approached politely – and is clearly shown to have not a leg to stand on – he/she may well do what you want and salvage some of their damaged reputation. If you write in too "stroppy" a manner, the recipient will actively look for a way to frustrate you. And work closely, in such letters, to the recommended framework. Be very business-like.

A letter of complaint along the lines of the following example would probably succeed:

Dear Sirs

INVOICE 8855709: THREE-PIECE SUITE

I was most surprised to receive a bill from you for re-upholstering my three-piece suite.

You will recall that I wrote to you on 12 April 19– – telling you how the original fabric had disintegrated within ten months of our purchasing the suite from you. As a result of that letter, one of your representatives called to inspect the suite and confirmed that there was a manufacturing fault in the fabric. He left with me the duplicate of his inspection report which clearly accepts responsibility for the defect. I enclose a photocopy of this report.

In your letter of 2 May you offered to re-upholster the suite free of charge. I enclose a copy of that letter too.

Your invoice however requires me to pay for the new cloth; all you are paying for is the labour. I cannot accept that, with a clear acknowledgement of a fault in the fabric, I should pay for either material or labour.

I am sure that this is no more than an administrative error. I am therefore returning the invoice herewith for cancellation.

Yours faithfully

In the above letter, the writer makes the subject clear from the start, by identifying the invoice number in the heading and reminding the reader of the past history. The introduction merges with the factual history as the writer goes on to outline his/her case – and encloses copies (never originals) of supporting documents. Finally, the writer gives the reader a way out – they can pass it off as a clerical error – but makes it clear that action is required.

It would be difficult to fault the tone of the letter; it is polite and restrained. If the facts are right a reasonable firm will probably agree to cancel the invoice.

Social letters

Social letters vary as much as does the population itself. You might wish to write a news-filled, gossipy, letter to a friend; an invitation to a party; a letter of congratulations or of condolence; or a love letter.

Lovers, I'm sure, need little advice on what to say in their *billets doux;* the only caveat is to be wary, should one party wish to avoid total commitment, and for possibly publishable *faux pas*. (I realise that I have gone against my own recommendations and used foreign phrases in that sentence. But French *is* the language of love – *n'est-ce pas?*) I am not offering a sample love letter. Write your own.

We have already commented on congratulation and condolence letters. And an example of an invitation letter was included in Chapter 1. All that leaves is the letter to a pen-friend.

For such a letter, the formal framework recommended in the Chapter 1 is not particularly relevant. There is much merit though in listing the items that you are going to mention, to avoid overlooking an important piece of news. As far as writing style is concerned, the basic recommendation that you should *write the way you talk* is even more relevant. The more you can "be yourself" and write the way you would perhaps gossip over a cup of tea, the more your letters will "come alive". Don't try to write differently from the way you chat.

In the next chapter we will consider, in some depth, the rather more specialised types of letters: sales letters, charity appeal letters (which are much the same), and Letters to the Editor.

Summary

1 Remember that the recipient of an unsolicited letter seeking help may be busy. Be brief – get to the point as quickly as possible – and be polite, to achieve the best results.

2 Address people by name whenever possible, rather than writing impersonally to a job title. Telephone and ask for a name to address.

3 When submitting a CV for an advertised post, endeavour to bring out one or two particularly relevant skills in the covering letter. If writing "cold", mention a mutual contact or acquaintance whenever possible, and make sure that you sell yourself quickly and efficiently.

4 The recommended framework for a letter is largely irrelevant for a letter of condolence. All that is needed is sympathy.

5 Be careful in writing a reference: it must be honest and helpful – yet need not exceed what is asked for.

6 A letter of complaint should never be written in the heat of the moment – or you may live to regret it. Plan such letters carefully and, initially at least, be very polite and even deferential. And make sure that you get all your facts right.

7 In social letters even more than in others, *write the way you talk*; be yourself.

4

SPECIALISED LETTERS

In the previous chapter we have looked at various everyday letters which many people find troublesome to write. Now, let us look at the types of letter which few people need to write other than occasionally; which when they do write, they particularly want to be effective; which are always difficult; and which have to be handled rather differently to those we have already looked at.

First, sales letters, and the basically similar appeal letters: both are seeking to part the reader from his/her money.

Sales and appeals letters

And the first thing to acknowledge is that some of the "rules" about good writing style are best forgotten when writing sales or appeals letters. Underlining is very much in, and so is the exclamation mark. Your first major objective is to get past the apathy barrier.

Let us look at some of the underlying principles that relate to sales and appeals letters. These are that:

- People are basically self-centred. To reach them, you have got to show them "What's in it for me?" And everyone loves a bargain.

- People have short attention-spans. You must make your sales pitch, your appeal, quickly – or lose the reader's interest. And the longer a sales/appeal letter is, the more likely it is to go into the waste paper basket. (Overcome this problem by using enclosures to expand on the basic letter.)

- People will react more favourably to a clearly spelt-out course of action. "Please complete the enclosed form and return it to me today" will certainly have more effect than "Think about this and let me know as soon as possible if you can help."

- People read headlines before (and sometimes rather than) the rest of the text. In a sales letter you can provide the equivalent of headlines by underlining the main points.

- Repetition, or near-repetition, helps to get the message across.

- The "rules" of *writing the way you talk*, and of short words, short sentences, short paragraphs and simple punctuation apply even more to sales and appeals letters than to other letters.

The basic framework which we recommended earlier for letters is largely still valid for sales and appeals letters. But it needs expanding and elaborating on.

The expanded framework for a sales or appeal letter can be expressed as a mnemonic, HIBA:

H – the *hook*. You need to grab the reader's attention quickly, before he/she can throw the letter away. You need to demonstrate that the letter is personally applicable – that there is something in it for him or her.

I – the *information*. Hit the reader with the basic facts: what you can offer, or what you want from him/her – and why.

B – the *benefit* – for the reader, personally. The answer to the "What's in it for me?" point. And there must be something.

A – the *action*. Tell the reader what to do – and how and when to do it.

And you can see how "H – the hook" represents the basic Introduction; "I – information" and "B – benefit" are the "Facts"; and "A – action" is the same as the standard letter framework's Action element.

Let us now see how the HIBA mnemonic works in practice.

Seeking donations

First, an appeal letter, seeking donations – which you might be asked to write for your local church. (Don't leave it to the vicar; he might not be "pushy" enough. But then again . . . ?)

Dear Muddlecombe Resident

MUDDLECOMBE CHURCH ROOF APPEAL FUND

Another begging letter, I can hear you say.

> **BUT WAIT!**
> Don't throw this letter away yet.

Let me explain why <u>this one</u> is different.

You are quite right, I am begging. Not for myself, nor for my favourite charity, but for you.

> I AM BEGGING – <u>ON YOUR BEHALF</u>.

What is the Trouble?

You enjoy living in Muddlecombe. Maybe you moved here to be "in the country". But what makes Muddlecombe the charming village it is? The old cottages, the winding lanes, the nearby fields and the view across to the Hills? Certainly, but it wouldn't be the same if the church had only a corrugated iron roof, would it?

* * * The Parish Church <u>IS</u> Muddlecombe * * *

"Don't be absurd," I hear you say. "A village church can't have a tin roof." But it can.

How Much is Needed?

Unless we can collect £20,000 – yes, TWENTY THOUSAND POUNDS – before the end of the year, we must either close down the church or protect it with the only roofing we can afford. And that means corrugated iron.

If we don't get the £20,000 the church will have to have a corrugated iron roof. And we shall have to live with that roof for at least ten years in order to recoup the expense.

What Can You Do to Help?

I am asking every one of you – long-term resident or newcomer, church-goer or non-church-goer, Anglican, Free Church or Catholic – to give as much as you can afford. And I need the money NOW. The alternative is a tin roof.

If you are generous to the extent of £200 or more – and I hope many of you will be – then your name will be recorded for posterity on your own, personal, brass plate fixed to the end of one of the church pews. But even if you can only afford a few pounds, your name and donation will be inscribed in a fine Roll of Honour book to be kept on permanent display in the church.

How Can you Subscribe?

Please complete the simple form at the foot of the page and send it, with a cheque or cash, to me, Maynard Friday, at the Rectory, Muddlecombe – TODAY.

Or you can phone me, NOW, on 63636 with your credit card number and I will arrange for your donation to be paid direct. (Not less than £10 by credit card please.)

And remember, for £200 your name will be recorded – permanently – on a brass plate on one of the pews.

PLEASE give generously. Think of the Muddlecombe skyline – with a tin-roofed church – and act NOW to preserve the heart of YOUR village.

Thank you.

Maynard Friday
St Swithin's Church

That appeal has quite a punch. It uses the HIBA approach – plus a few presentational gimmicks that would be out of place in many other letters (the underlined headings and text, the "boxes", the asterisked statement, the capitalised text).

The *hook* – the grabbing of the reader's attention – is quite a long one; it is also a bit "gimmicky" with its "don't throw this away yet" approach. But gimmicks pay off.

Throughout, the underlined headings encourage the reader to read on. And using questions as headings gives them a more personal feel.

Just about everything above the heading "How Much

is Needed?" is introductory *hook* – but with just a hint of the *information* to follow in the reference to the likelihood of a tin roof on the church. The boxed-in pronouncements would be totally unacceptable in any other type of letter – but they are right here. They are necessary to ensure that the "Don't throw this away, I'm doing it for YOU" message gets across. The next section, under the heading "How Much is Needed?" is mostly *information* – but also describes the main *benefit* by emphasising the disadvantage of poor quality re-roofing.

Under the heading "What Can You Do to Help?" the letter jumps to the *action* by asking everyone to give money now; it then swings back to offer a further *benefit* – a bonus, which always helps – in the form of public approbation. This again plays on the readers' self-interest.

Then, under "How Can You Subscribe?" the reader is given clear instructions on what to do and how to do it. Pay now, any way you like. (A separate payment form might have been an improvement, but separate forms cost money and church appeal funds have little to spare. So, a built-in form was probably the right compromise.)

Anyway, I think that if I lived in Muddlecombe I would probably succumb. And I'm no soft touch.

The same principles that have been applied to the appeal letter would be equally valid – but without the financial aspect – in a campaigning letter. Should you wish to muster the support of neighbours to oppose a new tower block development, or the support of like-minded people to campaign for "Teddy Bears' Rights" – or whatever – use the HIBA framework. It will work here too.

"Hard sell" letters

The church roof letter was seeking donations; let us look now at letters seeking to persuade readers to buy something.

The HIBA framework will still apply; so too will limited use of "gimmicks" and techniques otherwise frowned on. One technique particularly appropriate to a sales letter is the list. It is also appropriate to a business or technical report (*See* Chapter 6), but is usually out of place in a conventional letter.

It is always useful, in sales letters, to list the services, qualities or advantages of whatever is on offer. The listed items can then be emphasised with "bullets" or "blobs" in typing, a lower case O with the centre filled in. (I have used this listing technique several times in this book; being a "How To" book, the technique is appropriate. It would be inappropriate in a novel or a biography.)

Whether they are listed with bullets or not, one of the basic essentials of a sales letter is to identify the selling points of the product or service. If these are few, they may be better outlined in a more flowing description; if they are many, the list is almost always the best way of presenting them.

But the selling points should not just be listed in random order; some points are bigger, more important, than others. You need to start your list with a bang and, to ensure that you don't end with a whimper, end with another bang too. And in between, you need to bring the points out logically, building up the case for buying. (List the points on a sheet of scrap paper and re-arrange them – repeatedly – until you get the order right.)

Now, a sample. I recently helped to rewrite a sales letter for a writing colleague. Much of the basics of that letter would serve equally well to advertise my own services; for this book therefore, I have rewritten it as though for myself:

Dear [name]

Thank you for responding to my advertisement. You have taken the first step along the road to better business communication.

I can help with anything you want writing – for your business, for a charity organisation, or just for you. And I will do it well.

You may be happier with the sales or manufacturing side of your business than struggling to find just the right words for a sales letter or press release. Or maybe you just don't have the time to spare. I can relieve you of the burden – and let you get on with what you are best at.

Whatever you want, I will write it for you. Writing is my business. I am a skilled <u>wordsmith</u>.

I can offer:

- to write a hard-hitting sales letter for a mail-shot – like this one;
- to write the words for a sales brochure – and then go on to design it, illustrate it, and have it printed;
- to write magazine feature articles about your business – for use in advertising magazines;
- to write press releases – quickly and to order – for the launch of a new product or service;
- to write your annual – or any other special – report for you;
- to write a speech or provide the text and visual aids for a business presentation;
- to write you a new CV – for that change of job you so much want – and the covering letter to go with it; or
- to write anything else you may need: important one-off letters, minutes of meetings, etc. – anything. You name it. I'll write it for you.

I have plenty of experience as a wordsmith. I have published twenty books – several on how to write – and hundreds of feature articles in publications all over the world. I have written sales letters and brochures, speeches, presentation briefings, minutes of innumerable meetings and many business reports. And I have several years experience in personnel management.

I offer you a <u>personal</u> made-to-measure writing service. My fees are reasonable – I bill by the hour plus expenses – and I agree an estimate with you before I start.

Please write – or phone – NOW and let me take the writing load off your shoulders. I KNOW you will be satisfied.

Yours sincerely

In the above letter I have been somewhat less brash than in the church roof appeal letter. This was, of course, deliberate. I wanted to show how an appeal letter could benefit by being "gimmicky" – and how a sales letter could be "pushy" without using gimmicks.

The first point to note is that the sales letter – in this case, a response to queries arising from a small advertisement – is addressed by name. The reader is already a little bit hooked but needs "landing". So, I indulge in a rather soft *hook* to complete the process. "You've taken the first step . . ." And then, I give the reader an excuse to delegate the writing tasks which he/she may feel should be done personally: "You may be too busy . . .", ". . . let you get on with what you're best at."

From then on, explaining first that I am a wordsmith, the letter is into the *information* stage – which uses the list, with "bullets", to good effect. The list covers what I can (or would, were this for real) offer and ends with a nice "catch-all" item. Then, still at the *information* stage, I briefly outline my credentials for offering the service.

Throughout, the *benefits* of my relieving the client of some of his/her work-load have been emphasised, but now the other side is picked up. The reasonable cost is a decided *benefit*. (And even if the cost were high, I'd still call it a benefit.) But because I prefer to negotiate rates, I do not specify actual amounts. I don't want to frighten a client off before we meet.

Finally, the call for *action*. "Write or phone NOW." And a repetition of the immediate and direct advantage to the reader.

For other good examples of hard selling letters, look on your own door-mat, almost any day. We all scoff at the *Reader's Digest* or *AA/Drive* sales letters – "You, Mr Bloggs, are one of the very few people in Magnolia Street, Muddlecombe, who have been selected to receive this month's special offer . . ." But they are undoubtedly effective. Study them. Insurance companies too are getting very good at mail-shot letters.

One thing you will notice in some of the sales letters you get through your letterbox: the increasing use of the post-script. You may, like me, have been brought up to believe that a PS at the end of a letter is rather "bad form"; certainly it shows a lack of prior thought and planning. But it does have an impact, particularly if it is in the same – "strong" – handwriting as the signature.

We all know that many letters are drafted by someone other than the person signing them. A handwritten PS though "must be the real thoughts of the top person him/herself". (If you actually believe that, you'll believe anything.)

Without doubt though, a PS, preferably handwritten, has considerable impact in a sales or appeal letter. So use the PS gimmick – but make it short, and use it sparingly.

But now, off on a completely different tack.

Letters to Editors

For many people, to have a letter published in any newspaper is a major ambition. They long to write so effectively that their views and comments will be selected for publication. (Those who are only after a "soapbox" from which to air their prejudices though, will seldom achieve publication.) Many other people also write to Editors – but with the object of achieving *paid* publication. They are often freelance magazine writers learning their trade.

(Many magazines pay extremely well for Letters to the Editor. It is not uncommon for a published letter to earn its writer at least £5 and often £10. Even better, many magazines pay £20 to £30 for the "Letter of the Week/Month". These sums may seem small; but they are for very short letters: 100, or at most, 200 words. £30 for 200 words is *at the rate of* £150 per thousand words. And that's good payment for magazine-writing.)

And so, already, I have hinted at one of the basic rules of how to write letters to editors – keep it short. To expand on that, make your letters concise, easily read, to the point, and well-constructed; for magazines and tabloids, be personal, perhaps provocative, and if possible, slightly funny; for "quality" newspapers be sure that what you say is apposite – and logical. Above all, for all publications, be original; never copy someone else's letter or idea.

Make sure that you send the right letter to the right publication: a humorous account of finding Grandma's missing false teeth might be right for *Weekend;* it would be unlikely to achieve publication at *The Times*.

All editors prefer letters to be typed (but clearly don't insist) and on only one side of the paper, preferably A4 sized. Do not expect an editor to reply to your letter. If you achieve publication you are doing well.

(Paying letter "markets" may hold a letter for several months before finally deciding to use or not to use. So don't send the same letter elsewhere too quickly.)

As I have already mentioned, when I was collecting material for this book, I asked the editors of several newspapers, plus *Weekend*, for their advice on how best to get a letter published. All reinforced my emphasis on short simplicity. But it is also worth looking at some of the other points they made.

The Times, Letter Editor: "Obviously personal experience of particular topics helps to establish a writer's bona fides; humour helps; wit is less common but just as welcome. A good lean, tense, individual style is worth far more than a volume of waffle." The Letter Editor also mentioned that some people write to *The Times* several times a day. One person has written almost daily – for thirty years.

The Western Daily Press, Editor: "I would suggest correspondence be kept to a single issue wherever possible. We do get quite a lot of 'while-I-am-putting-pen-to-paper-may-I-also-raise-the-point' type of letters. These people may find it therapeutic to get a whole series of grouses off their chests, but inevitably they dilute the effect of their main complaint." The Editor adds that some letter-writers' use of technicolour pens and much underlining makes life very difficult.

The Southern Evening Echo, Deputy Editor: "We like brief, well-constructed letters, preferably typed. One point that might be of use – the supply of readers' letters tends to dry up at holiday times so the chances of having a letter accepted for publication are improved during those periods." The Deputy Editor adds that "silly" letters are frowned upon: "We are too busy to mess around with someone else's frivolities."

Weekend, Deputy Editor: "The only letters that stand a chance are those that are succinct, sensible and to the point. It does help sometimes if they are amusing too. What doesn't work is the gimmick letter – we get all shapes and sizes of them and they go straight in the bucket." (At the time of writing, *Weekend* pays £10 for each letter published and £30 for the best each week.)

Summary

1 The framework for a fund-raising or sales letter should be much the same as for any other letter – but expanded. It is best remembered as HIBA: the *hook*, the *information*, the *benefits*, and the *action* required.

2 In sales or fund-raising letters, underlining (and the exclamation mark) is widely used. The writer needs to grab the reader's attention very quickly.

3 Fund-raising and appeals letters need to appeal to the readers' self-interests, to answer the "What's in it for me?" question.

4 Readers need to be told very clearly just what action is wanted of them – and any payment facilitated.

5 Sales letters should list the goods or services offered and the benefits they will bring. All lists are improved by the use of "bullets".

6 If you wish to write a Letter to the Editor, keep it succinct, to the point and ideally, just a touch humorous. That apart, present your letter well.

5

GOOD-LOOKING LETTERS

As we have already remarked at the start of this book, it is not enough for a letter to be well planned and well written. It must also look good – be well presented.

Good presentation means more than good handwriting or fault-free typing – which are, of course, essential. It covers several more aspects of appearance, including:

- correct, and correctly placed, "tops and tails" (openings and closings)
- good setting-out on the (preferably single) page
- good quality paper – and envelopes
- an appropriate letter-heading, well printed
- if typed, a clean, fresh appearance (a fairly new ribbon)
- the right length (preferably not more than one page)
- how to start page 2 – if you must.

Let us now examine these points in detail.

Opening and closing letters

Other than in an internal office memorandum – and even there they cannot be completely overlooked – every letter needs a beginning and an end. And there are certain conventions that still need to be adhered to.

First, the conventional aspects. If you start a letter with a formal "Dear Sir", "Dear Sirs" or "Dear Madam", you must end it with the conventional "Yours faithfully". You should not round off such a letter with a "Yours sincerely". But everyone knows that these days.

When you adopt the vastly preferable "Dear Mr Smith" or "Dear Jane" approach for a business letter, you should always end with "Yours sincerely"; if the friendship is closer, a "Dear Bill" letter can end with just "Yours", "With kind regards", or "Best wishes". An even closer friend might end a letter with just "Love" – and not expect to have anything untoward read into such a phrase.

For the most formal of letters – to royalty, titled people, judges and the like – there are certain formal, time-honoured openings and closings that you might feel bound to adopt. These formal phrases can be found in many classic reference books; they are inappropriate in this book.

But there are other items, within the necessary opening and closing sections of any letter, which need to be considered.

The sender's address must, of course, be on the letter; increasingly, it will be printed thereon. (*See* Letterheads, below) If not printed, the address (and phone number) should be written or typed in the top right-hand corner of the page. Whether written or typed, it is preferable for the address to be in a neat block, each line commencing immediately beneath the other ("ranged"); it is acceptable though, but dated, to stagger the sender's address.

Every letter should of course bear the date of writing. In personal letters, written or typed, it is customary for this to be placed immediately below the sender's address.

In personal letters, the next item is the salutation – "Dear Mildred". Written or typed, this should be at the left margin, a line or two below the date line. The letter text then follows a line or two beneath that.

For "private business type" letters (which should preferably always be typed), with no letterhead, the sender's address and phone number (and perhaps the date) should ideally be in a "ranged" block in the top right-hand corner. With a letterhead, the date – the first line – is often at the left margin. Thereafter, letterhead or no, the layout of a business-type letter is more or less standardised.

A line or two below the date line, at the left margin, there may be a set of reference initials (the initiator's and the typist's: GG/KK). Beneath this, it is customary to type the addressee's name and address, again at the margin. A few lines beneath the address comes the salutation, "Dear Ms Baxter". A few more lines below that, comes the title (usually in capital letters) followed a line or so later by the letter text. (It is also acceptable, but slightly dated, to put the addressee's name and address at the foot of the letter. The top location is compatible with the increasing use of window envelopes; the foot-of-page location is not.)

The most commonly adopted format for the typing of a business letter is what is known as "blocked"; that is, each paragraph begins at the left margin, without an indent. It is also customary not to punctuate the date, the address, the opening salutation nor the closing endearments. (*See* Fig. 5.1 for opening and closing punctuation details.)

What You Need to Know . . .

        . . . About Punctuating Openings and Closings

Dates: The preferred way of writing the date is now "19 June 19—". Note that this is wholly without punctuation but the month and the year are shown in full. The next most popular way of writing the date is to put "19th June 19—" – but that takes two more key-strokes. Other acceptable, but somewhat dated (sorry) ways of showing the date are:

    January 23rd 19—   Jan. 23, 19—.   23 Jan —

Never date a letter in the form "10/6/—", "10-06-00" or "10.6.—". Although you may mean 10 June 19—, an American will always read it as 6 October 19—.

Addresses: On unheaded writing paper, you need your own address in the top right-hand corner with your telephone number below. The modern, preferred way is to block the address and omit all punctuation. It is also acceptable – but time-wasting – to punctuate fully. You can also – and this frequently goes together with full punctuation – stagger the start of each line of the address: Thus:

Preferred:	*Acceptable:*
16 Mill Road	16, Mill Rd,
Muddlecombe	Muddlecombe,
Mudds QE0 0QQ	Mudds. QE0 0QQ.
Muddlecombe (09893) 444	Muddlecombe (09893) 444

It is customary to type the addressee's name and address at the start of a business letter. This should always be "blocked" and may be punctuated, but preferably not. Here, you may use the titles Mr, Mrs, Miss, or Ms – customarily without punctuation – or merely the first name without a title. If you really must, use the title "Esq"; but never say "Mr W. J. Makepiece, Esq." – "Mr" and "Esq." together are quite wrong. And generally, you should avoid using the old-fashioned and rather class-conscious "Esq." altogether.

Opening: "Dear Sir" is fine without a final comma – or worse, a colon. The punctuation-free salutation goes with the preferred address styles above. With a punctuated address it is better to include the final comma – "Dear Sir," – but never use a colon.

Closing: With the unpunctuated blocked address etc., the "Yours . . ." requires no final comma. When the address etc. is punctuated, include the comma – "Yours truly,".

FIG. 5.1

Some writers persist however, with what is known as the "semi-blocked" format, in which the paragraph starts are indented but the addressee's name and address and the salutation are kept hard up to the left margin.

In all cases, blocked or semi-blocked, current practice is to leave a one-line gap between consecutive paragraphs. (You will seldom see any business letter at all today which does not have this space between paragraphs.)

The "blocked" format and the missing punctuation were originally adopted to save typing time; they are now retained on grounds of appearance – they give a letter an uncluttered look. Many "private business" letters too, now adopt the same layout, particularly the absence of paragraph indents.

At the end of the letter, the "Yours . . ." is usually preceded by a blank line. For personal letters, all that then remains is to sign. For typed "private business" letters it is helpful, and for business letters essential, to type the name, and where appropriate the official position, of the sender about six lines below the "Yours . . ." Again, all punctuation is usually omitted.

The preferred locations for opening and closing material – address, salutation, etc. – for a handwritten personal letter and for a "private business" one, are illustrated in Fig. 5.2. overleaf.

Page layout

We have already touched on the matter of page layout while considering "tops and tails" and format, above. But there is more to page layout than the mere placing of salutations etc. and whether or not to indent paragraph starts. A one-page letter should look good as a free-standing artefact.

MAJOR CHARLES SIMPLE-FRYTEFUL
ALDERSHOT COTTAGE. HONEYDUE STREET. MUDSHOTTE. MUDDS. MZS 1PP
09890 998

17 March 19—

My dear Geoffrey,

Thank you so much for your invitation to tiffin on Thursday. I'm very much afraid though that I mau'nt be able to come on parade that day. I've got t...
pm —
"half se...

Another...

Angela Merrywiddle Freelance Illustrator
Myrtle Cottage High Street Muddlecombe Mudds MZ9 9QA

Muddlecombe (09893) 492

25 June 19—

The Art Editor
Creative Spouse Magazine
XYZ Publishing
33 New Victoria Street
London SC2 9AY

Dear Lesley

Thank you for giving me the "Viewpoint" artwork to do for you. I enclose the final sheets herewith.

I am also taking this opportunity of sending to you, entirely on spec, a few of my other drawings of a more general nature. These might be of use for "fillers" in the magazine. I noticed that you have been using some thumb-nail cartoons like this, recently. Perhaps one or two of mine would make a change.

I look forward to hearing from you shortly – with the cheque for the "Viewpoint" stuff. I enclose the usual invoice. I shall also be most interested to hear what you think about the other material.

It would be nice to see you again. How about lunch at the Dog, next time I'm up in town?

Yours sincerely

Angela

Angela Merrywiddle

FIG. 5.2 Layout examples for two letters, one hand-written, one typed.

The most important consideration in making the page as a whole look right, is to centre the text.

Consider a sheet of A4 letter-paper. A neatly typed, well-written letter starts high up, immediately below the letterhead – and finishes no more than halfway down the page. Only narrow side margins are provided. The whole looks ugly and unbalanced.

Now think of the identical letter, re-arranged, and typed with generous side margins and with a gap between the letterhead and the start of the letter. The letter now sits more comfortably near the centre of the page. It all looks well-balanced and attractive.

Generous side margins have other – mundane – advantages too. First, they allow for the inevitable filing-punch holes, which do not then obscure the text; and secondly, they provide room for the recipient to make notes about how the letter is to be dealt with. (Fig. 5.3 shows (a) the bad, crammed together letter and (b) the same basic letter, presented more attractively.)

We have already mentioned the "blocked" layout – without starting indents for paragraphs. This is now commonplace. With the growth of electronic typewriters and word-processors however (*See* Chapter 7, page 119), it is possible to type letters with a "ranged", non-ragged right edge too. (This is achieved by the machine automatically inserting additional spaces between words, so that the typing fills the line from margin to margin.)

Because it can be done, it often is. But "ragged right" text is generally easier to read than text which is ranged at both left and right edges. The unusual, over-large, spaces between words are distracting. For typed letters, it is preferable to retain the ragged right edge.

Fig. 5.4 shows the same passage typed both ragged right and ranged – sometimes referred to as "right-justified".

Greene & Brownsocks (London) Ltd
73 Stocking Lane, London SC3 9PY   Tel: 01-888 0003/6
Registered office: 73 Stocking Lane, London SC3 9PY. Registered in London: 9876543.   UAT No. 123 45 6789

30 February 19--

The Sales Manager
Slim-waist Ltd
London S7 96QQ

Dear Mr Whistlestop

JAMES DUGLETS - Ref: TH/658/91
Thank you for your letter of 15 February, in response to our request for
a reference for Mr James Duglets. Your comments were most helpful. I
would like to seek a little further elaboration however. Mr Duglets has
told us that he rose within your organisation from being an assistant
salesman in your show-room to a position of Chief Area Sales representative for the whole of the south of England. I realise that job titles
are often a "moveable f────" but I would be most grateful if you would:
a) confirm that Mr Du[glets was promoted in the way he says, and b) give]
me some idea of the r[esponsibilities of the latter post. Please phone]
me if you would prefer [this.]

Yours sincerely

Rosemary Cottage (Ms)
Personnel Manager (Sal[es])

Greene & Brownsocks (London) Ltd
73 Stocking Lane, London SC3 9PY   Tel: 01-888 0003/6
Registered office: 73 Stocking Lane, London SC3 9PY. Registered in London: 9876543.   UAT No. 123 45 6789

30 February 19--

The Sales Manager
Slim-waist Ltd
London S7 96QQ

Dear Mr Whistlestop

JAMES DUGLETS - Ref: TH/658/91

Thank you for your letter of 15 February, in response
to our request for a reference for Mr James Duglets.
Your comments were most helpful. I would like to
seek a little further elaboration however.

Mr Duglets has told us that he rose within your
organisation from being an assistant salesman in your
show-room to a position of Chief Area Sales
representative for the whole of the south of England.

I realise that job titles are often a "moveable
feast" but I would be most grateful if you would:
a) confirm that Mr Duglets was promoted in the way he
   says, and
b) give me some idea of the responsibilities of the
   latter post.
Please phone me if you would prefer this.

Yours sincerely

Rosemary Cottage (Ms)
Personnel Manager (Sales)

FIG. 5.3 A crammed together, badly-laid-out letter – and virtually the same letter, nicely centred on the page.

```
It is customary today to use "blocked" format for typing
letters. This requires each paragraph to be started
without an indent. The absence of an indented start to the
paragraph might make it hard to determine where a fresh
paragraph begins. But it is also customary now to leave a
one-line space between each paragraph - which makes the
paragraph start easily identifiable.

There is also considerable evidence that typewritten
material left with a "ragged" right edge is easier to
assimilate than is typescript which has been "right-
justified". When a modern electronic typewriter or word
processor produces "right-justified" (that is, both left
and right margins straight) ordinary typescript, it does
this by adding spaces between the words, filling up the
space to the margin. The above two paragraphs are typed
with "ragged right" margin. They are repeated below, but
fully "right-justified" - the word processor does this
automatically. The margin settings are unchanged.

                .....................


It  is customary today  to use "blocked"  format for typing
letters.   This  requires  each  paragraph  to  be  started
without an indent.  The absence of an indented start to the
paragraph might  make it  hard to  determine where  a fresh
paragraph begins.  But it is also customary now  to leave a
one-line  space between  each paragraph  - which  makes the
paragraph start easily identifiable.

There  is  also  considerable  evidence  that  typewritten
material left with a  "ragged"  right  edge  is  easier  to
assimilate   than   is  typescript  which  has  been "right-
justified".  When  a modern  electronic  typewriter  or word
processor   produces "right-justified"  (that is,  both left
and  right  margins straight) ordinary typescript,  it does
this by  adding spaces  between  the  words, filling  up the
space  to  the margin.   The above two  paragraphs are typed
with  "ragged right"  margin.  They  are repeated below, but
fully  "right-justified" -  the  word  processor  does  this
automatically. The margin settings are unchanged.
```

FIG. 5.4 The same piece of work, first "ragged right" and then, by use of a word processor, "right-justified".

Stationery

Having looked at the way a letter is set out on the page, let us consider the paper itself. Letter paper can vary in size, thickness, quality and colour.

For business letters there is no question about size. Paper should be mostly A4; occasionally though, there is a use for two-thirds A4, or half A4 – which is A5.

And you can manage perfectly satisfactorily, as I and many others do, using only A4.

For personal letters of a business nature, there is also much to be said in favour of A4. If nothing else, it keeps the files tidy. And, of course, it *looks* business-like.

For purely social letters – to be hand written – a smaller sheet is often preferred: a 7-inch by 9-inch sized sheet is both popular and practical. If though, like so many people today, you type most of your social letters too, then you should again favour A4-sized paper.

Paper thickness and quality are closely linked. A high quality 100 gsm paper ("gsm" meaning grams per square metre of paper) is preferred by big, high quality, businesses. If you use the same quality paper, it suggests that yours too is a high quality business. (Or that you are extravagant.) If you use cheap, thin, poor quality paper it will inevitably create a "down-market" impression. (I use an expensive 100 gsm Conqueror "laid" paper for important letters, and a 70gsm Croxley Script bond paper for invoices and the like.)

It need hardly be said, but letter writing paper should never be lined; this despite the fact that for drafting letters or taking notes, most people use pads of lined paper.

The colour of your letter paper is a matter of personal choice. You will not go wrong with the whitest of white paper (often called "High White"). You may prefer a pale pastel shade; that's fine, even for "business" use, but be careful. Pale yellow, grey or blue are fine in any circumstances but a pale pink could suggest that a letter was from Barbara Cartland – which may or may not be your intention.

Remember too that, ideally, your envelopes should match your paper. White envelopes are readily obtainable; pink and stronger colours, probably not.

If you are writing business letters (or typed social

letters) on A4 paper then in most cases your envelope will preferably be DL-sized (4.25″ × 8.625″). A DL envelope is designed to be exactly right for an A4 sheet folded in three. Or – and particularly perhaps, for typed social letters – you may prefer to fold the A4 paper in quarters, for which a C6 envelope (4.5″ × 6.375″) is ideal. The DL envelope looks more business-like; the C6 envelope more "friendly". For hand-written social letters on 7″ × 9″ paper, there are matching envelopes ("Size 3") which accept the paper folded into three.

And, of course, for short, hand-written, social letters there is much to be said for the illustrated note-card, or "notelet". These are sold complete with matching envelopes. Just one note of caution here though: for convenience in mechanical sorting, the Post Office prefer envelopes to be no smaller than 90 mm × 140 mm (roughly 3.5″ × 5.5″) and oblong. Some note-cards may be too small and/or oddly shaped.

Letterheads

All businesses, and an ever-increasing number of private individuals, use headed notepaper. And, of course, as every letter has to have the sender's address on it, it makes little sense for this not to be printed. It is only the peripatetic nomad, the infrequent letter-writer and the genuinely impoverished who can justify *not* having printed notepaper.

Let us consider the individual and the business separately. First the individual. All that is needed on his/her notepaper is the address and telephone number; the name is not usually included.

It is a matter for personal choice whether the address and phone number are printed in mock script, in Gothic, in capital letters only, or in *sans serif* type.

Similarly, an individual can choose to have the address etc. central or on the right of the page, staggered or "blocked", or spread in a single line across the whole sheet. It will to some extent depend on the format you normally adopt for your letter writing. It would look a little odd to have a centred, Gothic heading and for you then to write in an unpunctuated "blocked" format. Similarly, the same paper would look odd if all social letters were typed.

For hand-written letters, a staggered right-hand corner address in plain type – with or without *serif* – is probably safest. And the phone number could well be printed in the top left corner.

When your social letters are almost always typed, there is something to be said for a very plain type spread across the top of the sheet. It takes up slightly less room and can be used as a guide for the typing margins. Some people like a printed line beneath such a letterhead, to separate it from the text. But again, the choice is all very personal.

For those individuals who, like me, effectively run a one-man business, the letterhead assumes a greater importance. In such cases, the name – preferably both first and family names, rather than mere initials – should always be included. (Never include "Mr", "Mrs" or "Miss". Nor, for my money, any past military title.)

There is also then the question of whether or not the letterhead should identify the business, trade or profession of the letter-writer.

I believe that too brash or blatant a letterhead is counter-productive. For one-person operations such as authors, freelance writers, artists, photographers, graphic designers I do not favour mentioning the profession or trade in a letterhead. I believe that the occupation becomes clear from the body of the first letter – and thereafter is unnecessary. But this is very much a personal view. Many successful colleagues add a discreet "Member of the Society of Authors", "Freelance Writer – NUJ Member" or "Photographer" to their letter heading.

Were I offering my personal services as a consulting civil engineer though – as I could but am not – I would most certainly include my professional qualifications "CEng, FICE" after my name in the letterhead. But I still would not, I think, add the words "Consulting civil engineer".

Maybe in this respect I lean too much towards the discreet "soft sell" But, in my experience, the bigger and more important the organisation or business, the more discreet the letterhead usually is. I take my line from that.

Home-made letterheads

The increasing use of word processors (*See* Chapter 7, page 119) has led to many people producing their own standard letterhead. They design what to them is an attractive layout and typeface (and size) and retain it in their computer's memory. Each time they wish to write a letter, all they then have to do is key in a short command and the machine reproduces the standard letterhead layout.

This can be suitable for personal letters but it looks unprofessional for business letters. Even – or even more so – from a one-man band.

If you do need to produce a personal letterhead on your word processor – maybe you feel you must, for reasons of cost – at least think carefully about the design. Many word processor users seem to use every font (typeface) available to them in designing their letterhead. Look at the letterheads of larger, well-known, companies; seldom do they mix the typeface –

sometimes the name is more emphasised, but never do they mix italic and Roman script in the same heading. The basic rule is to be as simple as possible.

If you want a separating line between letterhead and text, use a line (underlining); not a row of asterisks, pound signs, equals signs, or pluses; and never a mixture of characters. Differentiate between name and address by changing from 12-point type to 10-point, or even 10-point condensed. And a hint: you will have less trouble aligning the different-sized typefaces if you "centre" everything.

But "word-processed" letterheads are not the only alternative to a proper printed sheet. Many people use the little name and address stickers normally intended for the backs of envelopes. Again, this is perhaps acceptable with letters to friends – but never for business letters.

And the same advice applies – with even greater disapproval – to the use of a rubber stamp of one's name and address. Such stamps are invaluable for envelope backs (for return address) and for photographers to stamp the backs of pictures sent out for sale. But not for much else. (And to add insult . . . these rubber stamps are sometimes charged with green ink.)

If you want a letterhead – and if you are in business, you need one – get it printed. There is really no good substitute. (If you have a computer and printer and are prepared to invest in a desk-top publishing program (*See* Chapter 6, page 109–10), you might manage to produce a worthwhile heading; but it is not practicable to do this every time you want to write a letter.)

Business letterheads

Business letterheads are rather different from private, or one-man professional letterheads. Many businesses use both colour and black-and-white type in their heading, and it is also customary to incorporate the company *logotype*. The heading will of course include telephone and telex numbers. One or two firms – mainly in the computer or electronics business – are also starting to include details of how they can be contacted via electronic mail. (*See* Chapter 7, page 128) It is also necessary for the registered address – which may not be the same as the mailing address – of a public company and its registration number(s) to appear on the headed paper. There is also, in some cases, a legal requirement for the names of a firm's directors to appear on their notepaper. These, together with the registration details, are often tucked away in "the small print" at the foot of the page.

Big businesses employ graphics studios to design their writing paper. The letterhead will not be designed in isolation: continuation sheets, compliment slips, visiting cards, envelopes, report covers, the company news-sheet, product packaging and even all four sides of the company's lorries will often be conceived at the same time, as a single, integrated, design package. And where there are subsidiary companies, the stationery (and much else besides) will often be designed as a group exercise.

Many small and middling-sized businesses however, take insufficient care over the appearance of their stationery. Let us consider a few fundamentals:

- the name of the company must be clearly shown and must stand out from the rest of the essential information, address and telephone number(s) etc. which have to be included. A good basic type size for the address etc. is 10- or 12-point.
- the business of the company should be indicated.

(The initials of the world's biggest computer company are universally recognisable and its business immediately known. With Bertram Bloggs the Butcher, it is necessary to identify the trade. Bloggs alone will not suffice.)

- a *logo* (or logotype) is helpful – and the more it is used, the more identified, and thus the more helpful, it becomes. But make sure that the *logo* is unique to the business. To use a standard piece of "clip-art" – a butcher's apron, a cow, or a leg of pork or lamb – only cheapens the appearance of a letterhead.

- a letterhead should not occupy too much of the available (A4) paper. A quarter of the sheet is almost excessive; about twenty per cent is probably about right for a business letterhead.

- an estate agent, or property developer perhaps, might incorporate a stylised view of an attractive modern housing estate in his letterhead. Beware though: this has to be done very well, or better not at all.

- the printing itself must be of good quality. Nothing damns a letter more than faint or blurred printing – which is sometimes a result of using poor quality paper.

Examples of good and bad letterheads are shown in Fig. 5.5. (And for this illustration, some of the "type-setting" has been done using a simple desk-top publishing program.)

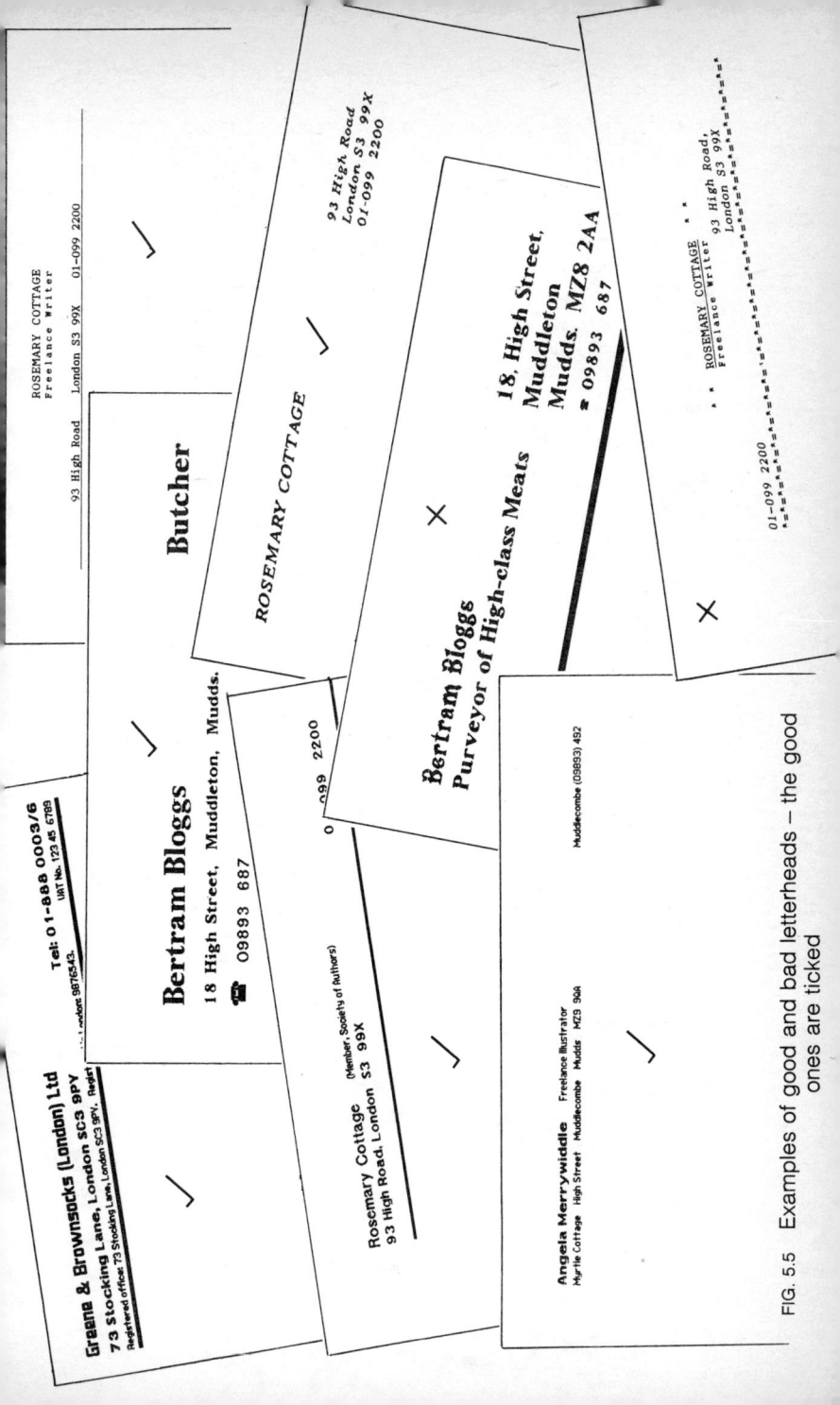

FIG. 5.5 Examples of good and bad letterheads – the good ones are ticked

Good typing (or handwriting)

In this chapter so far we have been looking at the standard "tops and tails" of a letter, the quality of the paper and the printing and the layout of the content. All this is to no avail if the content is not easily readable. I refer now to the quality of the typing or handwriting.

If your handwriting is difficult to read, or – a more subtle point – is not in keeping with your image, then don't write, type. If you can write neatly but your writing deteriorates when you are rushed, take time. If you want to send a handwritten letter, then it must be attractively and clearly written. (You might like to learn to write in the always attractive italic script; there are many short courses in calligraphy.)

But most of today's letters will, or should, be typed. And if typed, they must be typed well. Poor quality typing shouts of lack of care, incompetence – or pennypinching. These are bad images for a letter to convey.

Ways to ensure that your typing looks good include:

- maintaining even key pressures. On a manual typewriter, inexpert little fingers may strike keys less hard than do index fingers. Better still, upgrade to an electric, or electronic typewriter, or a word processor.

- setting the margins wide – "home typists" often seem parsimonious in their use of paper.

- maintaining a constant format. If using an indented paragraph start, maintain the (same) indent throughout; if leaving a single space between paragraphs, do not, for other than good reason, leave a double space.

- not overriding the right margin setting – "to squeeze the last word in". Go onto the next line. *Or* . . .

- avoiding over-long gaps at line-ends by judicious hyphenating of longer words. But do not overdo this. Too much hyphenating is, and looks, far worse than a moderately "ragged" right margin. (And be sure to hyphenate in the right place: usually between two "stand-alone" consonants, as in splen-dour but *not* in wit-hout; or after a vowel, carrying the consonant over – eg ana-lyse – but *not* so in words like dividing, which should be divid-ing.)

- cleaning the type-keys. Ensure that the enclosed letters are free of built-up gunge.

- avoiding too many "painted-out" alterations – avoid *all* handwritten alterations (if possible).

- changing the printer or typewriter ribbon frequently. This applies equally to manual and electric typewriters and to word processor printers. An over-faint typescript is hard to read – and makes the writer look mean.

Letter length

The length of a letter is an important factor in its appearance. It is also of course, as we have already discussed, an important factor in the way the letter is written (composed). Probably around ninety per cent of all letters – other than "chatty social" or "business legal" – need be no more than a single page.

You should strive to restrict every "non-chatty" letter to a single sheet. A concept, proposal or thought which cannot be expounded in a single sheet is probably not sufficiently well thought out. It is said that, during the Second World War, Sir Winston Churchill insisted that even major strategy papers put to him for consideration should not exceed a single page.

A single sheet letter is shorter than a Churchillian paper. It has to include the "tops and tails". The body of a single-sheet letter therefore needs to be held down to about three hundred words. Skimming through my own correspondence files for the last few years I found very few letters (in or out) which exceeded this single-page limit. But there were some.

When a letter needs to continue onto a second sheet, thought has to be given as to how to handle this.

First, a letter will appear badly planned if the only material on page 2 is the "Yours sincerely" and the signature. One way around this – if the letter cannot be slightly rearranged or shortened to fit into the single page – is to space out page 1 liberally, and move to page 2 earlier than would otherwise be necessary. There should, as far as possible, be a whole paragraph on page 2 above the signature block.

Secondly, the second page should ideally be on a specially designed sheet of continuation paper. This would perhaps be a page with just the sender's name or *logo* at the top. Whether the continuation sheet is printed or not though, it should be of a similar quality to the top sheet.

Thirdly, the second page should carry identification of the continuing letter. Letter pages can easily become separated; an unidentifiable page 2 is of little value and can be a considerable embarrassment. The top of page 2 should therefore carry the name of the person to whom the letter is addressed, the date, and the page number. And if continuation paper is not used, page 2 should also carry the name of the sender. My own practice is to type something like:

spread across the top of the (plain) paper, often underlined, and with three or four lines of space beneath, before continuing with the letter. Another practice, economical in typing time when used with a printed continuation sheet, is to type the addressee's name, followed on the next line by the date, and on the following line, "Page 2". These three lines are ranged left, at the top of the sheet with several lines of space beneath them, before the text continues.

And remember, the object is to make the page *look good*. Where a letter runs onto two pages, the second page must look as good as the first.

Summary

1 It is most important that a letter should *look good*. This goes beyond the mere content to embrace the way it is set out, the quality of notepaper, the printing of the letterhead, the layout of the page, and how well it is actually written or typed.

2 There are standard words and layouts for opening and closing letters; the *latest* conventions in these matters should be adhered to. Old-fashioned looking letters do the sender no good at all.

3 Ideally, type all letters – even social ones – and lay them out well. Modern convention is a "blocked" style without paragraph indents but with a line space between paragraphs. Allow generous margins at all four sides. Preferably, type with a "ragged right" margin – rather than "right justified".

4 Printed letterheads – even for handwritten personal correspondence – are preferred, generally on the

best possible quality of paper. Ideally, envelopes should match. Business type letters should be on A4 paper.

5 Subdued and "restrained" letterheads are usually the best. "Home-made" letterheads are to be avoided as far as possible – even when your word processor will produce an "acceptable" one. The printing should be of the highest quality possible.

6 The typing (or handwriting) of a letter is very important: it must *look good*. One of the worst "sins" is to use a tired ribbon in a printer or typewriter.

7 Strive to restrict any letter (other than "chatty social") to a single page. If you must expand onto two pages, provide an identification note at the head of page 2.

6

GOOD-LOOKING REPORTS

The content of this book is not restricted solely to the craft of writing effective letters. At work, you will often have to write reports, as well as letters. Some reports may only be a page or two long; others can be longer.

All the earlier advice about planning your writing, and how to develop a good writing style is just as applicable to reports as it is to letters. Perhaps more so. Reports need to be carefully planned; they need to be clearly and simply written; and they need good presentation. And it is in their presentation that reports differ most from letters.

A business letter will usually have a title; it will seldom warrant further sub-headings. A report can seldom manage without "chapter" (or section) headings and sub-headings – and for a report, the concept of a whole hierarchy of headings needs to be considered. (*See* Chapter 1.)

A good business letter will seldom exceed a single page in length. Few reports can be that short. And because they are longer, reports need more planning – to get the *balance* right, between different sections. (We have already introduced and recommended the concept of a word budget in Chapter 1.)

A good business letter is like a well-framed picture. It sits centrally on its single page. The open space around the text, which makes the letter look so fresh and easy to read, comes almost inevitably. The layout of a report needs more and specific attention. And the intended layout may influence the way you write the report.

A business letter would not, normally, be illustrated. A graph or small table is generally out of place in a letter. But most reports will benefit from tables, graphs and other illustrations. (Remember the old editorial comment about a picture being worth a thousand words. But remember too that this adage only truly applies to a good picture that "says" a lot.)

A business letter, even in these days of sophisticated electronics, is usually produced in fairly standard typescript. Some reports are designed (yes, and that too) to be properly printed.

The basic text – the "body" – of a business letter, being short is, in its context, complete in itself. Because of its length, its "stand-alone" nature and often, its complexity, a report almost always needs a summary, usually a contents page and sometimes even an index.

Let us look then at how a report can best be presented. We need to consider:

- length
- content and headings
- layout
- illustrations
- production.

Report lengths

We saw, in Chapter 1, how important it is to think about the length of a letter, or report, before you write it. The best length for a report is . . . as long as it needs to be. The guiding principles of concise simple writing still of course apply. And we have seen how a word budget can help to ensure a proper balance of content between different elements of the report.

But the length of a report will also affect the way in which it is to be presented. A single-sheet printed and illustrated report, even if double-sided, will still *look* like a throw-away leaflet. It may be better to produce it in typescript. Or maybe the size of type can be changed to make it appear bigger. (Publishers, for instance, regularly adjust the size of the print to make a short book appear longer.)

And early thoughts about the length of a report will enable arrangements to be made for its production. A long report will require more preparation than will a short, simply produced one.

Report content and headings

Visualise a business/technical report. It will usually have a cover; forget this for the moment. Inside, there will be a title page, a contents page, then a summary (or maybe these two will be reversed), then several chapters or sections, and finally perhaps, a few sheets of plans, tables or diagrams. It may be all typewritten or it may be properly printed, with glossy photographs even.

The need for the title page is obvious. Readers need to know what the report is about. For shorter reports, not sub-divided into sections or chapters, of course, the title can be merely at the head of page 1.

Why a contents page though? Business readers are busy people. If the report is of interest to them – and they will soon dispose of it, if it is not – they will need to refer to some sections more than others. Different readers will have different primary interests; each may be most interested in just one of the several chapters. The contents page is a quick guide to allow the reader to *return* to the particular section of the report which most interests him/her. Without a contents page, a report is a maze.

To be effective, a contents page needs to list, not just the chapter or section titles, but also the sub-headings within each section. Think of a section of a report as the equivalent of a chapter of a book. Turn to the front of this book, and look at its contents page; notice how both the chapter titles and the headings within each chapter are listed. This is what – perhaps differently set out – a report contents page should be like.

Continue to look at this book's contents page. Notice how the title of each chapter makes clear its single-subject content: planning, writing style, sample letters, appearance, etc. Notice too how the sub-headings within chapters clearly identify the content of each relevant section.

If, from the contents page alone, you wanted to relocate what I had said about sentence lengths, this would be straightforward: Chapter 2 – Writing Style; fourth section – Short simple sentences. And if, as often in reports, the number of the page on which each heading appears is given, I can go direct to the required advice.

In writing a report, make sure that you give similarly helpful titles to your chapter/sections and subsections. There are few things more frustrating than a report in which the headings are over-generalised. Consider, for example, "Introduction", "The Main Report", "Appendices". Yet headings such as these are not uncommon.

A further aid to moving around within a report – which is inappropriate in almost all letter writing – is the numbering of paragraphs. (My cautious reference to paragraph-numbering in letters is because it is customary, in many government departments to number paragraphs in both external and internal correspondence.)

Report paragraphs can be numbered simply (1,2,3,4 . . . 99) in sequence throughout a complete document or within chapters, or they can be numbered, decimal-fashion by section- or chapter-heading and sub-heading (1.1.1; 1.1.2; 1.1.3; 1.2.1; etc.). In short reports, simple numbering is recommended; in longer reports, say over four typewritten pages long, the decimal approach is recommended.

To elaborate on the use of the decimal paragraph-numbering system, consider a report – on a housing development proposal – divided into four main sections. Section 2 is entitled "The Proposed Development"; it has three sub-headings within it, named "Location of Site", "Development Proposal", and "Implementation Proposal"; and within the first sub-heading there are two paragraphs. The numbering system is then:

2 THE PROPOSED DEVELOPMENT

2.1 Location of Site

2.1.1 Describes the site location.

2.1.2 Refers the reader to a relevant illustration.

2.2 Development Proposals

2.2.1 Para

2.2.2 Para

    etc.

2.3 Implementation Proposal

2.3.1 Para

    etc.

When using the decimal paragraph-numbering system it is necessary to have a sub-heading immediately following the main section heading. Thus, in the above example, one could not write introductory paragraphs within Section 2, before 2.1.1. You should not have 2.0.1. If you need to write a general opening paragraph, you will have to introduce this with a further sub-heading: "2.1 Introduction" and renumber the "Location" sub-section as 2.2. (This differs from the practice when writing most non-fiction books, when an opening heading immediately below the chapter title is generally unacceptable.)

A final point to bear in mind when establishing a set of report headings and the numbering system is that, once established – for a given report – it must be adhered to. Once you decide that your report is to have sections, and within the sections, sub-headings, then you should not, while writing, suddenly decide to put in a sub-sub-heading.

Similarly, and to jump the gun on the (next) section in this chapter on layout, once the *style* of the headings is established, this too must be adhered to throughout. (By *style* I mean, chapter headings in plain capitals, sub-headings in underlined lower-case typescript. You must not, in mid-stream, change the sub-headings to bold lower-case or the chapter headings to underlined lower-case – or even underlined capitals.) This happens all too often.

Report layout

The points about paragraph numbering and heading *style* in the previous section are matters of layout as well as content and headings. Which leads us into the overall question of layout.

The layout of a report has much in common with the

layout of a good business letter. Big margins are still desirable; and I would myself still favour a "ragged right" margin. A one-line space should always be left between paragraphs – but the "fully-blocked" unindented paragraph start is no longer always strictly appropriate. This will be obvious by the earlier reference to the merits of paragraph numbering.

There are two common approaches to paragraph layout in reports. Both are compromises. In one approach the paragraph number is hard up against the left margin but the first letter in the paragraph is indented by perhaps 10 spaces from the margin. Thus:

> 4.6.24 The start of the actual text is indented to, say, ten spaces from the margin but on subsequent lines, the text "ranges" on the number.

The approach is to use a "reverse indent", whereby the paragraph text is fully "blocked" but the number projects into the margin. Thus:

> 4.6.25 The actual text maintains a "ranged" left margin but the numbers project into that margin.

There are clear advantages in both approaches: the reverse indent enables speedy location of a numbered paragraph but has a somewhat ragged appearance; the "half-and-half" approach looks neater and is more economical in paper, but is less easy to operate.

The reverse indent method is easy with a word processor, but fractionally less so with a typewriter (you need to "tab" each line after the first). Using the "half-and-half" method on my word processor entails my "tabbing" in for the start of the first line; the reverse indent is fully automatic. Other words processors will differ.

Reports have identification and page-numbering requirements too, much like those of multi-page letters. But the solution is usually different. Not all report-writers bother with identifying individual pages, but everyone numbers them.

A preferred method of identifying both report and page number is to use what in word processing is called a "header". The report typist programmes the computer to include, at the top of each page, some such phrase as "North Bank Development" and a page number. (I am using precisely that system in writing this present book.) It is equally possible to have the "NBD" title at the top and the page number at the foot of the page (a "footer"). The words and/or numbers can be located at left or right of the page as required. Bear in mind too, the need to leave sufficient blank space between header and text and between text and "footer" to differentiate. My personal preference is for a single "words and numbers" header at top right.

The layout of a page of typescript is not just a matter of margins, indents, gaps between paragraphs, and page numbering. Each of these have their place. And one of the major results of these layout elements is to generate space.

Space – blank space – is what makes a page look bright and easy to read. A century ago, newspapers used tiny headlines and few illustrations. The whole effect of such pages on a reader of today is one of dull heavy greyness. Today, we all expect our reading material to *look good* – and that means looking bright and airy. Brightness on a typed or printed page is created by the space around the words. The wide margins and the space between paragraphs help but the more extra *space* you can create, the better the report page will look.

The shorter your paragraphs are, the more frequent are the spaces between them. Thus, you kill two birds with each short paragraph: your writing becomes easier to read and the page layout is improved. In business reports, you can also create extra *space* by using occasional tables – there will be space around a small table – and lists.

Lists are particularly appropriate in reports:

- they offer a quick way of absorbing linked information;
- they enable otherwise over-long sentences to be shortened;
- they are attractive – particularly if used with "bullets";
- they create *space* around the list – particularly if the listed items are short (which these are not).

But now glance back at the list at the start of this chapter (page 100). There, the listed items were short; the blankness of the surrounding space is considerable. When typing a list, the typist should leave a blank lane above and below the list, even when, as is customary, the list is within a paragraph. An extra *space* bonus.

Lists are appropriate in most technical writing. Notice how often I use them in this book; they would not be appropriate in, for instance, a biography. They are not really appropriate in, for instance, a company chairman's report – but they would be very much so, in an internal report to the same chairman on a new company project. (They are also very useful in sales letters, as shown in Chapter 4: for much the same reasons.)

Illustrations

Like lists and tables, illustrations generate *space* in a report. In most day-to-day reports illustrations mean little more than graphs, pie-charts and/or bar-charts. But these minimal illustrations are very valuable. They convey information painlessly (or, at least, they should), they break up the text, they generate interest (What do *you* look at first, when you pick up a book or report?), and again, they create *space*.

One thing to watch out for in report-writing is the production problem of fitting illustrations into the "run of the text". With the possibility of easy textual amendments above and below it, even modern word-processing facilities cannot always readily ensure that an illustration is visible at the same time as the whole of a related paragraph. Some reports banish all illustrations to the back. And that precludes many of the potential benefits.

A further point to watch when illustrating a report is to ensure the suitability of the drawing. Too often one sees a map or scale drawing merely photo-reduced to A4 (or perhaps a fold-out A3) size. And this is quite unsatisfactory. Lines and lettering appropriate to a large map or plan, when reduced in size, are seldom sufficiently big or clear. The lines will be too thin, the lettering hard to read.

Illustrations for use in a report should be purpose-made; designed to be read at A4 size. And to be understood, they may need to be simplified.

Production

Most letters are written for one addressee only. Reports however, are often expressly intended for wide circulation; many copies will be needed. The production of such quantities needs to be considered; it is not something which can just be "left to the typing pool".

The production of an effective report requires consideration of:

- printing method (photocopied typescript or printed – including possible use of desk-top publishing techniques)
- paper quality
- binding and cover.

Most reports will be photocopied typescript. We have already considered the layout of the typescript including the possibility of a "header" on pages after the first. The advice in the previous chapter about using a fresh printer ribbon is even more applicable to the preparation of a report "master" (from which copies are to be made). Longer reports can be photocopied onto both sides of the paper; this will entail adjusting the right-hand location of the "header". (Some word processors provide for headers to be sided automatically.)

Some word processors include typefaces which are virtually indistinguishable from typeset work. A "camera ready" master can be produced from which the reports are printed directly.

Another approach is to use one of the increasingly sophisticated desk-top publishing programs now available for personal (and of course, bigger) computers. The quality of the "master" produced from a desk-top publishing program is also a function of the associated printer. A 24-pin dot-matrix printer will produce a passable (but not outstanding) master. (The mock letterheads in Chapter 5 were produced with the simple NewsMaster II program on an Amstrad PC1512 computer linked to a Star NB24–10 dot-matrix printer.) A more expensive laser printer however, will produce a perfectly acceptable master. But the use of a desk-top publishing program is seldom justified for an in-house business report. Typescript is perfectly acceptable.

The paper on which an in-house business report is produced will to some extent be governed by the paper which the photocopier will accept. This is usually 80 gsm (grammes weight per square metre of paper) which is quite acceptable. But it is possible to feed a photocopier with thicker (heavier) paper – which might be preferable for an important report.

The need for a cover for a report will depend on its nature: a small-circulation, short (5–10 page say), internal report probably needs no cover at all; an equally short report which is to be widely circulated, and retained by recipients for frequent future reference, should probably have a strong cover.

Covers can range from a plain stiff card with a cut-out window displaying the title on the typed sheet below, to a pictorial glossy; from a simply lettered thin card with an overlay sheet of plastic to a full-colour artistic design on laminated board. And the binding too varies similarly. The first choice for a small report is, of course, simple stapling down the edges of the sheets. Available binding techniques then move upmarket, through the plastic or wire "comb", the saddle-stitched (like a magazine) staples, to the squared-off, "perfect", glued binding (as used for paperback books). Each has its place; the choice depends on the end purpose.

And of course, if the report is such that it warrants proper printing and full-colour illustrating, the cover and binding must suit this type of production. Here, edge stapling will not suffice. And vice versa.

Summary

1 A report needs as much care over its presentation as does a letter; the general approach is identical for both letters and reports; the details vary.

2 In most reports, paragraphs should be numbered – the decimal system (eg 2.4.1 etc.) is recommended – and there should be a sufficient number of within-chapter (or -section) sub-headings. These should be reflected in the contents page – which is the way to find your way around in a report.

3 A hierarchy of headings and sub-headings should be established at the start of report-writing, and conformed to throughout the preparation process. Similarly, a decision has to be made about how the paragraph numbers will be displayed; there are (at least) two acceptable methods.

4 The layout of any report will be improved by the use of more blank *space*. *Space* can be generated by the blank line between paragraphs (and the frequency of this, by the length of paragraphs), the width of margins, by illustrations, and by lists.

5 Lists are particularly valuable in report-writing – they look attractive, are easily assimilated, and generate fresh-looking *space*. Use "bullets" (●) for listing items.

6 The physical production of a report is important; a

report has as much need as a letter to *look good*. To achieve that, go for thicker paper if possible, move "up-market" from simple side-stapling, and consider the design of the cover.

7

OTHER WRITING MATTERS

Whether your main interest is in writing better personal letters – letters that get noticed – or more effective business letters at your workplace, you may one day need to write other things. A report for the local newspaper of your village football match or art exhibition perhaps; or maybe a user manual for a computer program or game you have devised. As a wage-slave, you may be asked to write a press release or an advertising feature article.

Fear not. The principles of good writing, which have been outlined earlier in this book, are equally applicable to all forms of writing. If you can write a good letter – and you can, now – you ought to be able to write a competent anything else. But you need to know some of the tricks of the trade.

You must not expect full instruction or advice here, on how to write press reports, press releases, user manuals or advertising (or other) feature articles. There are several helpful books on such writing; there is a list of useful further reading later in this chapter. But for now, let us look at a few guidelines on how to make a start at writing other than letters and reports.

Writing for the press

Both press releases – often little more than free advertising in disguise – and reports on a bridge competition or art exhibition for your local newspaper are based on the same principles. First, the principles you already know:

- Think about what the reader wants to know, or will be interested in.
- Don't write at all unless you've got something worthwhile to say.
- Arrange your points so that you start off with a "bang" – seize the reader's attention quickly.
- Write the way you talk. Make sure that your writing is clear and simple.
- Write in short words, short sentences and short paragraphs – with simple punctuation.
- Rewrite – cut out all waffle and pomposity – and polish. Then read it aloud to yourself.

If you follow those "rules", your writing will always be competent; but that alone is not enough when writing for the press.

For press writing there are certain extra rules that must be adhered to if your work is not to go straight into the "round file". You must:

- Make sure that you have got something – no matter how small – that is really *newsworthy*.
- Type everything you send to an editor. (And avoid "fancy" typefaces.)

- Submit news reports or press releases exclusively on plain white A4 paper. For a press release it is often helpful to submit on your business letter-paper. Immediately beneath the letterhead, type PRESS RELEASE.)

- Type double-spaced. (That is: type a line, miss a line, type a line . . .) Indent paragraphs by five spaces. You need not leave an extra blank space between paragraphs.

- Keep it short. A 200-word report or release has much more chance of being published than does a 500-word piece. And a 2000-word press release has no chance at all.

- Write so that you get the important points across first. Press releases and reports are often trimmed to fit the space available. The Editor will just "edit out" your words as necessary, from the bottom up.

- Provide a contact name (first name and surname, not initials, not "Mr", nor "Mrs") and phone number for further information – and be there.

- Wherever possible – name-drop. Mention the names of anyone with a local connection, and provide brief quotes from anyone relevant. Target the local interest.
  (And the same principle would apply to a press release or report for a national but specialist publication: mention names known within that field and target the specialist interest.)

- Be factual – and correct. Avoid opinion or comment absolutely. Leave that to the Editor.

- Provide a short title or heading, in capital letters, not underlined. (Don't underline anything – it means *italics* to a printer.)

- At the end of the report or release, put a line of dots and the word "END", in capital letters. The contact details go in beneath that.

If you feel the need to try writing a feature article for a magazine or newspaper the principles are much the same. We will look at the few differences below. And if your boss asks you to write an advertising feature article, that will need the same treatment.

How then does a feature article differ from a press release/activity report? Basically, a feature article is longer and is unlikely to be chopped about by the editor. It will either be accepted or rejected. The writing style should be as for letters or for other press work: clear and straightforward.

The most important difference is the even greater need for an article to grab the reader's attention quickly – and hold it. A reader may read a news story (within which category press releases purport to belong) because the headline seized his attention and because the item is short. He/she will abandon a longer article if it doesn't come up to expectations. There is no captive market in magazine readers. You interest them, or they don't read. And if your magazine article does not convince the editor that it will interest the readership, it will be rejected.

(There is a caveat to that edict though. If you are writing a feature article for use in a free-circulating advertising publication, your firm may be paying for it to be used. Unless it is truly awful, it will therefore be published. If that is the situation, you should though, for your own satisfaction, at least try to make it interesting and readable. That is, follow the same advice as that for general feature articles.)

Points to watch in producing feature articles, which

differ from those for press releases, etc., and relate mainly to layout, include:

- Unless given a specific length, aim at an article of no more than 1000 words. And 800 words is probably even better.
- Work to an average paragraph length of 50–60 words with a maximum of 80 words. Keep sentences short – an average of 15–16 words – and avoid all long words which are hard to understand. Just as for letters.
- Try to think of a catchy title – and keep this down to about four words. But don't be too clever in the title.
- Type, double spaced, on one side only of white A4 paper with big margins. Start on page 1 with the title (in capital letters) about half-way down the page and your name (in lower case characters) a couple of lines below. Don't underline the title or your name.
- Provide a header on each sheet after the first – in article-writing it is called a "strap" – consisting of a key word from the title, your surname, and the page number.
- Provide a cover sheet, giving the title, your name, the approximate number of words (to nearest hundred) and your name (again) and address. Put your name and address at the foot of the last page too.
- Submit the article, with a brief covering letter – merely saying "I enclose an article called TITLE for your consideration for publication at your normal rates. I also enclose a stamped addressed

envelope." And don't forget the sae. Then forget all about it. Get on with something else. The editor is NOT just waiting for your article; he/she has more important things to deal with.

- If you are writing for a covert advertising spot, you can expect better treatment from the editor. He/she may well wish to discuss your material – after all, you're paying for it to be used.

- A relevant black-and-white photograph will often increase an article's chance of being accepted. (No, not of you – unless you are asked; of whatever you are writing about.)

Writing a manual

If you are in the business of producing anything which is to be used – a tool, a piece of equipment, a computer program – the customer needs instructions. Someone has to provide a user manual. And if – like many in the computer world – the manual is badly written, the customer will be dissatisfied.

If you are the expert who has designed the new *gizmo* or written the wonder-program, you ought to be the best person to explain its use. Too often though, experts are poor communicators. But if you have absorbed the advice earlier in this book on how to write effective letters, you have a head start. All of the letter writing principles apply to writing a user manual – only more so.

A user manual is more like a report than a letter. Its content needs particularly careful planning. And to plan effectively, as always, you need to put yourself in the position of the user/reader. The reader may well know next to nothing about this new possession. So think simple. And start right at the beginning. There is much to be said for starting with something like, "In the box you will find . . . The big . . . is the . . . There are also two . . . s. These have to be screwed to the . . ." And so on.

There is little danger of being accused of "talking down" to the reader. The user who knows what to do will probably ignore the manual – or at least the early pages. The person who reads from page 1 will probably be delighted with your simple idiot-proof approach. I know I would be.

As with a report, and as recommended in Chapter 1, consider the advantages of setting yourself a word budget. It is a lot less daunting to think about writing 500 words about how to change a *wotsit* on the *gizmo* than to contemplate writing a whole, comprehensive, 20,000-word manual. And when it comes to the actual writing, write it in these smaller, manageable "chunks". Even if you get stuck on one section, there will always be another which you *can* write.

With a user manual, even more than with a report, it is also essential to think about illustrations. The "doing it" photographs and the diagrams are the reader's first port of call in search of help. Make sure that any photographs are close-up, well lit with good contrast, and set against a blank or unobtrusive background. Diagrams should be kept simple: almost cartoon-like. Include only such details as are necessary to serve the purpose of the illustration.

Word processing

Throughout this book, there have been references to the joys of word processing. A modern word processor is to a manual typewriter as the biro was to the quill pen. A word processor is probably the easiest way to ensure that your writing is *right* – before it gets onto the page. Yet many people are scared to make the change.

(The cost is a different matter. Word processors are still expensive. But a basic "Amstrad" (the Amstrad PCW8256) costs under £400 and comes complete – save for your fitting a plug on the cable – and ready to go. If you write a lot of letters, in your one-person business for instance, you can't really afford not to get one.)

A brief description and explanation of a word processor may help to allay the fears. The section which follows is an abbreviated extract from the chapter on word processors in my book, *The Book Writer's Handbook* (Allison & Busby, 1989).

So, just what is a word processor? The name has come to mean the full set of equipment whereby the user can type at a standard keyboard, see the resultant words instantly on a screen before his/her eyes, amend and correct them at will, store (and retrieve) them electronically, and then print them onto paper as and when necessary. But the equipment is really a computer (plus a printer) capable of several other uses; and the word processor itself is just a set of electronic instructions to the computer.

The whole concept of word processing is more easily accepted if the equipment itself is understood. Every word processor consists of the same items:

- a computer – the electronic gadgetry which interprets the instructions of the user.

- a keyboard – like the front part of any ordinary typewriter but with some extra keys.

- a monitor – just like a television screen – sometimes referred to as a VDU, meaning a visual display unit.

- a storage device – nowadays this is usually a disk

drive, which is much like a record-player; two disk drives are better than one.

- a printer – capable of receiving electronic instructions from the computer and transferring them onto paper.

- a word processor – a computer program (spelt correctly without the double-m, e, to refer specifically to instructions used in a computer).

The computer

A computer – the *central processing unit*, the CPU – handles instructions and information as a collection of "on" or "off" notifications. Think of millions of switches; they can each be either on or off. A computer "reads" each item of information in the form of eight switch-instructions; each number, each letter, and each punctuation mark can be expressed in a sequence of eight ons and offs (more usually thought of as 0s and 1s, in *binary* code). Each such 8-digit item of information is called a *byte*.

A computer has a memory: those millions of switches. The size of its memory is measured in bytes (sets of eight "switches") – or, more usually in thousands of bytes, known as *kilobytes*, or just K. The Amstrad PCW 8256 has a built-in memory (sometimes called RAM, meaning Random Access Memory) of 256 kilobytes. 256K – hence the model number (8)256.

As we are only really interested in the computer's word-processing ability, we could translate that memory size of 256,000 bytes into roughly 28,000 ordinary everyday words – and the space around them. But part of the computer's memory (its RAM) is used to hold its program of instructions. Allowing for the program, you may well have room for only say 10,000 words – but this is quite enough. You need hold no more in memory than just what you are working on immediately. And few letters – or even report sections – are 10,000 words long.

When you stop work – and also, for safety, at intervals whilst working – you have to "save" your electronic work onto disks (*See below*). Once "saved", your work cannot be lost by the computer – although of course the disks could be physically destroyed or lost.

Keyboards and monitors

To use your computer at all, you need a keyboard, on which to type. A computer keyboard is like a normal typewriter keyboard. But computers need extra keys. Every computer keyboard will have the all-important "Enter" key, a delete key or keys, and a means of moving the cursor (*see below*) around the screen. There are other keys but they will vary from machine to machine.

The "Enter" key – which could initially be confused with the conventional typewriter's "New line" key – is used to activate instructions to the computer and at paragraph ends. With a word processor you need never again worry about the end of the line – the computer reads your input as a series of paragraph-length lines which it then displays on the screen as normal typescript. You just set the margins you want, and the computer moves your words on, from line to line, automatically. And you see it all happening – on the monitor.

Just like a TV screen, a computer monitor displays the action. Before you start to type the screen will display what is called the *cursor*. The appearance of the cursor will vary but it is often a small upright oblong, the size of one typed character. The cursor tells you where your typing will appear on the screen. Touch any key. The initial cursor position will have been taken up by the character you keyed in, and the cursor will have moved one space to the right. Continue, and you form a word on screen.

Monitors can be dark green with paler green "writing" like the PCW8256 or black with white characters or, like some business word processors, a pleasant amber. Alternatively, the screen can be in full colour with underlined characters perhaps showing up in red, italic characters in green and bold in yellow. Some people find a full-colour word-processing screen like this rather distracting. And monochrome screens are cheaper.

Storage

As mentioned above, the work you put into your word processor computer must be "saved" before you stop work – and also at more frequent intervals to prevent accidental loss. The program (below) allows you to do this. But you need a storage device. Today, this storage is almost universally one or more disk drives.

You can have a single disk drive, from which the program is read in, and out to which the work is saved; you can have a pair of drives, one of which is usually used for the program and the other for saving onto; or you can have what is called a hard disk drive plus a single (floppy) disk drive. This latter set-up lets you hold your program permanently within the computer on the very large capacity fast-access hard disk to which all your work is also saved; and you can make extra, safety-first, copies onto a smaller-capacity floppy disk on the other drive.

Think of computer/word processing storage as

recording music on blank audio-cassettes. You insert a blank disk and "record" your new work onto it; next day, you can play it back, make corrections, and re-save it. And you can buy ready-made disks – the program – which you use in your work. The words you write on the screen are recorded on the disks in the form of electronic "blips" (representing ons and offs, or 0s and 1s).

The storage disks come in various sizes. The PCW8256 uses special 3-inch disks; some newer computers use 3.5-inch disks; most others use 5.25-inch disks known as "floppies" – because they are. All of these disks are removable from the machine and are stored separately. The hard disk referred to above is installed permanently in the computer; it is not removable. In all cases though, including the hard disk, once work is saved to the disk it is as safe as, for instance, a cassette recording. The computer can be switched off without fear of loss.

Printers

It is all very fine composing your thoughts onto a monitor screen, via a keyboard, and then saving them onto floppy or other disks. Eventually, even in these electronic days, you will still need to produce words on paper. And that means you need a printer.

Computer printers come in three main types, dot-matrix, daisy-wheel, and laser. The laser printer turns out work of exceptionally high quality, much like a photocopying machine. But its cost puts it out of normal reach. Most people must choose between a daisy-wheel printer and a dot-matrix printer.

A daisy-wheel printer operates in much the same way as a conventional typewriter – certainly as an electronic typewriter. Individual characters are moulded on the ends of thin arms fixed to a central hub. It is called a daisy-wheel because it is thought to look like a daisy.

The wheel is spun, under "instructions" from the computer, to place the appropriate character directly in front of the next space on the paper. A tiny hammer strikes the wheel's arm onto an inked ribbon which in turn hits the paper and marks it with the required symbol.

The quality of typescript produced with a daisy-wheel printer is identical with that produced on an electronic typewriter.

A dot-matrix printer works in a completely different way. A row of fine pins project from a printing head. As each character is needed, the computer program instructs the print head which pins are to project out against the inked ribbon and onto the page. Each character may be made up of several upright rows of pin marks – dots. Early dot-matrix printers used nine pins in a matrix perhaps 7 or 9 rows wide. The characters so formed were universally "dotty", but the machines operated fast.

In order to improve the quality of dot-matrix printing some machines offer a double run of the printing head. On the second run, the head is slightly displaced from its original position and the pin marks fill in the gaps left on the first run. This is known as near letter quality (NLQ) printing. The quality is variable, but usually quite good; it is readily distinguishable from daisy-wheel printing though. (Newer, more expensive, dot-matrix printers use 24 pins and produce typescript which looks as good as that from a daisy-wheel. The typed examples of letter layout in Chapter 5 were produced on a 24-pin dot-matrix printer.)

The Amstrad PCW8256 comes complete with a 9-pin dot-matrix printer. The newer, costlier, Amstrad PCW9512 has a daisy-wheel printer.

The word processor program

All of the word processing equipment however – in computer jargon, the "hardware" – is only as good as the instructions which make it work. The instructions are in the program, otherwise known as the "software". In the PCW8256 package there is a program called Locoscript. It takes a bit of learning but once you are used to it, it is very "powerful" – more computer jargon for "you can do a lot of different things with it". Indeed, many people never get around to using all of the facilities available in Locoscript.

If you invest in an Amstrad PCW8256, you do not need to consider the program to use, you have one. If however you are looking for a bigger, more robust, more versatile set of equipment, you will need to think about the program.

When investigating the purchase of a separate word processor program, it helps to know what facilities might be available and which are most useful. In my view, a word processor should offer:

- WYSIWYG – meaning *what you see is what you get*, and nowadays almost universally available.

- The ability to insert, delete, or transfer characters, words, phrases or paragraphs anywhere in the document which is then readily (or better, automatically) rearranged.

- A facility for changing the margins at will, at any spot in a document.

- The ability to draft, and print out, in single-spaced typing, and then, if needed, readily to change to double-spaced typescript. Or vice versa.

- The ability to write a *file* (jargon for a document)

of up to say 5000 words (45K) length and to move from one end of the document to the other without delay.

- A "macro" or "glossary" feature enabling the user to produce commonly-used phrases, addresses, etc. on screen (and into memory) with just one or two key-strokes.

- An ability to store, and call up as necessary, various different page layouts – eg, for business and/or private letters and for articles.

- An on-screen rolling word count.

- A built-in spelling checker. At the end of a document, you should be able to call up a check on the spelling – and be offered suggestions for corrections or be able to incorporate your own "new words".

- An on-screen indication of the end of each page – and the ability to "force" a page-ending at will.

- The ability to merge files together – for instance, to add more material to the end of a letter by incorporating part of another file (part of another letter perhaps).

- The ability to print individual pages from within a multi-page document.

Most word processor programs will offer most of the above facilities; before selecting a program you must check which are of most importance to you and which you can sacrifice for some other "goody".

Electronic mail ("E-mail")

There is one final aspect of letter writing which has not yet been touched on in this book. It is now possible to send correspondence electronically, by telephone. This is called electronic mail – often referred to as "E-mail". E-mail can best be thought of as a set of electronic pigeon-holes with telephone links to senders and receivers.

An e-mail subscriber (Yes, you need to subscribe to one of the operating systems – British Telecom's Telecom Gold is probably the best known e-mail system in Britain.) sits at his/her computer. The subscriber types in a message; the message is transmitted, down the telephone line to a large central computer; at the centre, the message is directed into and stored in the electronic pigeon-hole of the addressee; the addressee checks with the system from time to time, and is told that there is a message waiting; the addressee gives a personal password and the message is transmitted down the phone line to his/her computer. The message is displayed on the screen and if necessary, can be printed out.

E-mail is faster than first-class post – "delivery" can be made within seconds. E-mail is more reliable than telephoning – a full message can be left, rather than an ignorable request to phone back. E-mail allows the sender to prepare a carefully worded message "off-line" and then transmit it quickly – the addressee's "hard copy" (printed version) is more precise than notes from an off-the-cuff phone call. E-mail can, at a small sacrifice in delivery time, be used more cheaply by transmitting pre-prepared messages in off-peak periods.

To use e-mail, you need a bit more electronic equipment than merely your word processor. In all, you need:

- a computer, complete with keyboard, screen and – sensibly – a printer;
- access to a telephone socket;
- an all-important *gizmo* known as a *modem*: an abbreviation of "modulator-demodulator" which translates the computer's electronic output into audible signals which can be sent down a telephone line – and then, at the receiving end, translates them back into electronics;
- a communications program – the software; and
- a membership subscription to an e-mail system.

E-mail is here. E-mail is growing. But it can still only be used by subscribers; and by no means every person with whom you might wish to communicate is yet a subscriber. The literary quality of much e-mail often seems poor; not enough attention is paid to spelling and grammar, let alone to style. And there are certain conventions in "topping and tailing" e-mail "letters". If you get into the system, these are soon learnt.

You need to be aware of the existence of e-mail. For some while yet though, knowing will suffice. Back then, to the everyday world of words on paper.

Books about writing

There are many books about letter writing. Most of these are somewhat dated in their approach. My objective in this book has been to describe the *process* of effective letter writing and not, as many of the older books do, to give lots of examples to copy. Further advice on *how* to write particular types of letter, reports, etc., more effectively is available. Usually, this advice is contained within books on broader aspects of writing, management, or selling.

Some of the books which I find helpful – including some of my own, which incorporate more comprehensive advice on other than letter writing – are:

Robert Gunning: *The Technique of Clear Writing* (McGraw-Hill Book Company, New York) 1952. My favourite book on writing style; written by an American and mainly directed at business or press writing – but a very good basic approach.

J A Fletcher & D F Gowing: *The Business Guide to Effective Writing* (Kogan Page, London) 1987. The sections on writing style are very good.

L A Woolcott & W R Unwin: *Mastering Business Communication* (Macmillan, London) 1983. Good on the structuring and layout of business letters.

Mel Lewis: *Writing to Win* (McGraw-Hill Book Company, Maidenhead, England) 1987. Marvellous on sales letters, press releases and general presentation – even if at times a little too "pushy" for my taste. (I would, for instance, take a lot of persuading to use a photograph of myself on my letterhead – as Mel Lewis recommends.)

Michael Bland: *Be Your Own PR Man* (Kogan Page, London) 2/e 1987. Good on the general principles of selling yourself and on the specifics of writing press releases.

John Mitchell: *How to Write Reports* (Fontana,

London) 1974. Good on its subject. Rather technically oriented.

Gordon Wells: *How to Communicate* (McGraw-Hill Book Company, Maidenhead, England) 2/e 1986. A well-received book on the whole range of communication techniques: writing, reading, speaking, listening, and combining all these techniques in meetings; and how to communicate using visual, electronic and numerical techniques. This present book is an expansion of a small part of *How to Communicate*.

Gordon Wells: *The Successful Author's Handbook* (Macmillan – Papermac, London) 2/e 1989. Not about writing letters but much of the advice contained in this book – about writing non-fiction books – is also particularly relevant to the writing of reports and user manuals.

Gordon Wells: *The Craft of Writing Articles* (Allison & Busby, London) 1983. If you get into the business of writing press releases or feature articles (either general interest or for advertising) this book will be helpful.

Summary

1 If, as by now you can, you can write an effective letter, you can probably also write a competent press release, news report, feature article, or user manual.

2 Anything written for the press must be typed, double-spaced, on white A4 paper with big margins all round. And remember to get to the point quickly – and then hold the reader's attention throughout, just as with an effective letter.

3 A word processor is a highly desirable item of writing

equipment – but for purely personal use it is not cheap. A word processor allows you to get your writing right, on screen, before committing it to paper.

4 A word processor consists of a computer, a screen, a keyboard, a storage device, a printer – and the most important part of all, a program which controls all of these.

5 Electronic mail is effectively a bank of electronic pigeon-holes linked to users by telephone. To use it, you – and your addressee – need to be subscribers to an e-mail system such as Telecom Gold.

APPENDIX

Hints – For Writing Even More Effective Letters

- Keep carbon copies (or run off an extra word-processor print, in draft letter-quality) of your letters. This will allow you to read them aloud, at your leisure, to check on the style, and improve the flow, of your writing.

- When you have worked hard to get a paragraph *just right*, keep a copy of it – and use the same wording again, in similar circumstances.

- Keep in mind the possibility of using a handwritten compliments slip instead of a formal letter. It will be quicker and may be all that is needed.

- When answering a letter, read this carefully – to ensure that you answer *all* the queries. (Or omit the odd answer deliberately.)

- Before writing an important letter, list all the points you need to make – to ensure that none is overlooked.

- When inviting someone to call on you, who may not know the location of your home or office, consider sending a photocopy of a personalised (and simplified) map.

- If the copies of your letters are filed in an overall

office system, away from your desk, consider keeping a further copy of each of your letters, in date order, to facilitate immediate response to telephone queries about them. The person phoning will have your letter in front of him/her when phoning; you will not. He/she will assume that you remember everything you wrote; if you write many letters, you will not.

- The appearance and content of every letter you sign is *your* responsibility. Don't blame the typist or secretary; *you* should have noticed any errors before despatch. Never let an important letter – they are *all* important – go out with manuscript alterations in it. Retype it.

- Be lavish with blank space around your letter-text. The more blank space, the better the letter looks.

- Think carefully about the degree of informality you have adopted in each letter. To be formal to a friend is as bad a fault as to be too informal in the wrong business context. But, within those constraints, informality is generally to be preferred to formality.

INDEX

Active statements, 36
Amstrad PCW8256, 120
"And", 37
Appeals letters, 63–68
Articles, writing, 116

Balance, 21, 99
"Blocked" letter format, 79
Bullets, 69, 107
Business letterheads, 90
"But", 37

Capitals, use of, 37
Circumlocution, avoiding, 38
Clarity of (writing), 27
Closing letters, 78–81
Complaint letters, 59
Computers, 121
Condolence letters, 54
Congratulations letters, 58
Content, 5, 13, 101
Contents page, report, 101
Counting words, 39
Cover, report, 110

Daisywheel printer, 124
Dashes, 35
Decimal system for numbering paragraphs, 103
Desk-top publishing (DTP), 109
Disk drive, computer, 123
Donations, seeking, 65
Dot-matrix printer, 124
Draft, hand-written, 39
–, write in, 39

Editors, Letters to, 73
Effective letter, Qualities of, 2
Electronic mail (E-mail), 128
Ellipsis, 35
Envelopes, 86

Fog Index, 41
Framework for sales/appeals letters (HIBA), 64, 69

Gunning, Robert, 26, 41, 130

Handwriting quality, 94
"Hard Sell" letters, 69
Headings, 22, 101, 102

–, hierarchy of, 102
HIBA framework for sales/appeals letters, 64, 69

Illustrations in reports, 108

Jargon, 36
Job advertisements, letters responding to, 47
– applications – "cold", 49
Justification (margins), 83, 85

Keyboard, 122

Latin, use of, 36
Layout, page, 81, 104–108
–, report, 99, 104–108
Length, letter, 95, 99
–, paragraph, 31, 117
–, report, 100
–, sentence, 29
Letter, effective qualities of, 2
Letterheads, 87–93
Letter length, 95, 99
–, openings and closings, 78–81
Letters, love, 61
– of complaint, 59
– – condolence, 54
– – congratulations, 58
– – reference, 56
–, openings and closings, 78–81
–, presentation of, 77–98
– rejecting offers, 52
–, sample, 43–72

– seeking a job, 47, 49
– – donations, 63, 65
– – help or information, 44
– selling a product, 46, 63–72
– – yourself, 46
–, social, 61
– to Editors, 73–75
Lists, 34, 69, 107
Logo, 91, 92
Love letters, 61

Manual, user, writing, 118
Margins, 83, 95, 105
Modem, 129
Monitor, 120, 122

Numbering paragraphs in reports, 103

Openings (and closings), letter, 78–81

PS, 72
Page layout, 81
Paper, 85, 110
Paragraph numbering, 103
Paragraphs, short, 31
Passive statements, 36
Planning, 5–24, 99
Polishing, 39
Post-script, 72
Presentation of letters, 77–98
– – reports, 99–112
Press releases, 113
–, writing for, 114
Printers (WP), 124
Printing, report, 109

Production of report, 109
Program (WP), 126
PR work, 4, 113
Publishing, desk-top, 109
Punctuation of letter openings and closings, 80
– simple, 33
Purpose, 3, 5, 10–13, 25

Qualities of effective letter, 2
Questions, ask rhetorical, 37

Reader, 5–10, 25
Reading aloud, 40
Recipient, 5
Reference letters ("references"), 56
Rejecting an offer, 52
Report content, 101
 – cover, 110
 – headings, 101
 – illustrations, 108
 – layout, 104
 – length, 100
 – presentation, 99–112
 – production, 109
 – structure, 18–21
Reports, 4, 18, 99–112
Responding to job advertisements, 47
Ribbon, printer/typewriter, changing, 95

Sales letters, 63–72
Sample letters, 43–72
Second page of letter, 96
Seeking a job – "cold", 49
 – help or information, 44
Selling yourself, 46
Sentences, short, 29
Simple punctuation, 33
 – writing, 27
Social letters, 61
Space, 32, 99, 106
Stationery, 85–87
Storage (WP), 123
Structure, letter, 5, 14–18
 –, longer documents (reports, etc.), 18–21
Style, writing, 25–42
Summary, report, 101

Title, 22, 99
Tone, writing, 36
Tops and tails, letter, 78–81
Transparent writing, 26
Twain, Mark, 27
Typing quality, 94

Underlining, 34

VDU (Monitor), 120, 122

Word budget, 21, 99
Word-processed letterheads, 89
Word processing, 119–127
 – – typefaces, 109
"Write the Way you Talk", 27, 64
Writing a manual, 118
 –, books about, 129
 – for the press, 114–118
 –, hand, quality, 94
 – style, 25–42
 – tone, 36
 – transparently, 26